Bringing the Mother with You

BRINGING THE MOTHER WITH YOU

† *Sources of Healing in Marian Meditation*

BY RONDA CHERVIN
AND MARY NEILL

THE SEABURY PRESS · NEW YORK

1982
The Seabury Press
815 Second Avenue
New York, N.Y. 10017

Library of Congress Cataloging in Publication Data

Chervin, Ronda.
    Bringing the mother with you.
    1. Mary, Blessed Virgin, Saint—Meditations.
I. Neill, Mary.   II. Title.
BX2160.2.C53   232.91   82-13534
ISBN O-8164-2358-X   AACR2

All biblical references are to the Revised Standard
Version of the Bible: Old Testament Section, copyright ©
1952; New Testament Section, First Edition, copyright ©
1946; Second Edition © 1971 by Division of Christian
Education of the National Council of Churches of
Christ in the United States of America.

Contents

Who Are We?

I am Mary Neill, a Dominican Sister of San Rafael, California. After teaching in parochial high school for some years, I did my doctoral studies in France, focusing on the relationship between religion and psychology. I teach religious studies at the University of San Francisco and give workshops and classes throughout the West in journal keeping, pastoral ministry, and dream work. I have for four years been director of the comprehensive seminar for the Master's in Spirituality given by the University of San Francisco. My first book, coauthored with Ronda Chervin, was *The Woman's Tale*.

I am Ronda Chervin, an associate professor of philosophy at Loyola Marymount University, wife, mother of three; coauthor of *The Woman's Tale* and author of *The Church of Love, The Prayer and Your Everyday Life Series, Christian Ethics and Your Everyday Life,* among other publications.

Introduction : *Images of Mary*

Bringing the Mother with You

BY MARY NEILL

There is a Tibetan meditation on the mothers which helps in times of stress for refuge from the nonnurturing world. As I understand it, you bring to consciousness the notion that everything that exists has been mothered-forth. Millions of mothering creatures through the aeons have brought forth life, given it form and sustenance, guarded it fiercely against danger and decay. Then you call upon all that energy of these mothers to renew your sense that you are not alone in the struggle to survive — all the mothers guard you, child of the universe.

Such consciousness of archetypal energies awaiting our tapping seems to me to be contained also in the Catholic tradition of the devotion to the mysteries of the rosary.

Through now long ages millions of men and women have fingered their beads, murmured "Ave" over and over trying to give form to their joy and pain and ecstasy through meditating on the mystery of pain and joy and glory in the life of Jesus and Mary. And as they prayed, some healing touched their soul — some heart cure gave them hope and courage as they sank into this murmuring mantra. They found refuge for their sorrow: They had summoned the mother; they were not essentially orphaned and alone. "I will not leave you orphans," Jesus promised, and surely the rosary has been a "mother thing" for millions of Christians.

"Mother" themes and scenes abound. I read of the execution of tough Maoist soldiers who had survived the Long Walk, yet who cried "mother, mother" as they died. I think of Jim Jones' last words— "mother, mother, mother." I think of the pioneer mothers who against incredible odds brought their children and husbands through many a Death Valley. They endured and helped others endure.

We call for unconditional love in the face of our inner and outer deaths. Our belief that this unconditional love sustains and heals is the theme of this book. We must bring the Mother with us; the feminine principle that is the connection to the past and to the future; a connection that can encompass disconnection, disease, disharmony.

The oldest art objects found are squat figurines of what is called a "Venus Mother," heavily breasted and bellied, often with no head or face. The fertile earth Mother—breast and lap—evolves to the heavenly Mother—heart and eyes and hands. That evolution, too, takes place within us as we move from earth to air. Is the Mother we need for our times and the future to be one of fire (to purify the unchained passion and violence of our times) or of water —to dissolve our hardness against the feminine and the divine? "And the walls come tumbling down."

Bringing the Mother with You

BY RONDA CHERVIN

When Mary Neill first devised the title, *Bringing the Mother with You*, I was horrified. It seemed to imply that everyone had to carry their mothers on their backs, a burden so great that there would be no energy left to be oneself.

Then after Mary explained what the title meant to her, I began to think about all the warming images the word "mother" brings to my mind: a cozy, comforting bosom, delicious food, home. Next came happy memories of my own experiences as a mother: the mysterious presence of the baby within the womb, breasts flowing with milk for the tiny mouth of my son, arms encircling my twin girls as they snuggled close to me to be read to or to be comforted in pain. An African word for mother translates "she who hears when I call."

Finally I thought of my present transition to middle age. For me the physical burdens of mothering my family are almost over. At the same time I have climbed the career ladder quite enough. My goal now is to become a motherly figure to all. This means being more in the background yet very much present to affirm the goodness in others, to emphathize with their agonies, and finally to release them to the world. This is my own mother at her best. This is what I want to be. This is Mary—the Eternal Mother.

Writing this book will be part of my journey to the fullness of my motherhood.

Reader Response:

There is a section at the end of the book with topics for personal exploration alone or in a small group. You may choose to reflect on these questions after each chapter of our writings or meditate on all of them after reading the whole book.

The Face of Mary

BY MARY NEILL

The first face to fascinate us as infants was that of our mother. Her eyes and smile taught us to focus our vision, to arrange our face. How we trust the world, others, ourselves, depends in large part on what we saw mirrored in that face. As we borrowed our flesh from her, so we borrow our face. Finding our own individual face means many rebirths, many separations, from the first mother and other mothering persons and groups — and each leaving causes pain, as did our first leaving of the womb.

We long to bring the best of our mother with us — her willingness to give life — that we may become life-givers. The process whereby we leave our mother's face and heart and life-giving to find our own is a sacred journey, a process of transformation from physical to metaphysical, from outwardness to inwardness, from human to divine.

The Nahua Indians in Mexico believe that we are born with a physical heart and face but that we have to create a deified heart and a true face. The phrase used to describe the face we must make signifies a process in which heart and face combine. Our heart must shine through the face before our features reflect our deepest selves. Thus heart-making and face-making are two aspects of a process which creates in us a firm center from which we operate as human beings.

The face and heart of the Blessed Mary, mother of Jesus, has for centuries given Christians a model for the divinized face and heart we seek. She is the mother of joy, compassion, endurance, who stands before the fall of her world, who loves unconditionally her son, criminal or not. Suffering and joy find in her a steady center. She is present to herself, her Son, the world.

Though the nineteenth-century faces of Mary often present her as a Victorian innocent, the Middle Ages abounds with stories of her "naughtiness" — upsetting bishops, sneaking sinners into heaven, wiping juggler's sweaty brows in church. She is ever the compassionate one who, when there is a clash between Love and Law, makes sure that Love always wins.

Millions of tongues have murmured "never was it known that anyone who implored your help or sought your intercession was left unaided." What a powerful mothering consciousness we have in the face and heart of Mary. What a challenge to love ourselves and others unconditionally.

As we live in a world that seems less and less nurturing, it seems necessary now more than ever to meditate on Mary, to move deeply into our own unconscious to make connection with the arche-

6

typal images of Mother within — a connection made so much easier in times past.

My hope is that this book will help ease the making of connections, will personalize and translate the traditional meditations on Jesus and Mary so that the readers may be strengthened in their arduous journey to find and unite their true face and heart.

The Mysteries of Mary

BY RONDA CHERVIN

We bring the mother with us not only by contemplating maternal qualities but also by bringing the mothering consciousness with us in our life tales.

But how do we develop this mothering consciousness? How do we overcome the temptation to withdraw in the face of another's needs?

To have a mothering consciousness we must bring the mother with us, letting the maternal warmth we have experienced affirm us and then release us to mother others. Many of our childhood experiences, however, have been less than satisfactory. Some important needs may have gone unmet leaving us feeling deprived and therefore insecure with the maternal in others and the need for the maternal in ourselves. Our mothering consciousness thus goes underdeveloped. Our attempts to mother may be marred by doubt, fear, or anger.

One traditional way of developing our mothering consciousness has been to meditate on how Mary, the mother of Jesus, transformed her sorrows and joys. Her story in scripture and tradition has been condensed for us in the mysteries of the rosary, which have nourished generations of Catholics.

Of late the image has dimmed. We will be contemplating the mysteries afresh in the chapters to come. As we dwell on each of the joyful, sorrowful, and glorious mysteries of Mary's tale, we will be exploring the way our own lives embody the same themes: joyful surprise, confirmation, celebration, homecoming, crying out, violence, resignation, pain, the wound of death, reunion, ecstasy, fire, the leap to heaven, and the fullness of the end-times. We will sing Mary's song so that we can become sensitive to the new, the painful, and the overwhelming.

But before we plunge into the mysteries we should say something about the rosary itself. The rosary is a string of beads consisting of five sets of decades with ten small and one larger bead. A crucifix with two large and three small beads is added. Each decade is associated with a mystery of the faith, fifteen in all, which we have taken as our chapter headings in this book. The rosary is prayed by saying the Creed while looking at the crucifix, then praying the Our Father while holding onto the first bead; Hail Mary's for the intention of faith, hope, and charity on the three small beads; another Our Father and then Hail Mary's on the decades, punctuated by an Our Father on the large beads. During the praying of the Hail Mary on the smaller beads the meditation takes place on each of the mysteries within the joyful set (Annunciation, Visitation, Nativity, Presentation, Finding in the Temple) said on Mondays, Thursdays, and Sundays during joyful seasons of the liturgical year; the sorrowful set (Agony, Scourging, Crowning with Thorns, Carrying of the Cross, Crucifixion) meditated on during Tuesdays, Fridays, and Sundays during Lent; the glorious set (Resurrection, Ascension, Descent of the Holy Spirit, Assumption, Crowning of Mary Queen of Heaven) prayed on Wednesdays, Saturdays, and Sundays after Easter. The mysteries of the rosary can be found at the end of this book for those who might be unfamiliar with praying the rosary.

The question of the origin of the rosary is disputed by historians. It dates back at least 700 years and is particularly associated with the Order of Saint Dominic, and also with the apparitions of Mary such as Lourdes and Fatima.

Three ways of praying the rosary popular in our times are:

1. Praying with the beads in hand using the Our Fathers and Hail Marys as a sort of "mantra," that is, a repetitive prayer for

centering the consciousness. Many Catholics carry a rosary in their pockets or purses and pray in this way at odd moments of the day. Others keep it under the pillow and touch the beads during the night particularly as a way of bringing their anxieties to the Mother.

2. Praying the rosary as a conscious meditation on the fifteen different mysteries. Using this method the words of the Hail Mary and the Our Father become a chant and the spirit is focused on letting the meaning of the mystery infuse consciousness.

3. Praying the scriptural rosary as a means of letting the words of both the Old and the New Testaments add richness to the contemplation of each of the mysteries.

Many Catholics pray the rosary alone. Many others pray it with groups after Mass or in special gatherings devised for that purpose. Praying the rosary is also often combined with prayers of intercession.

I, Ronda, began to say the rosary as a sort of spiritual bargain. A friend of mine who married a non-Catholic told me that her husband converted immediately after she made a vow to pray the rosary every day. Jealous of her success and eager for the same results with my husband, I quickly made the same vow. My immediate reaction was chagrin since I rather disliked the rosary, associating it wrongly with Catholics whom I thought to be superstitious in their piety. However, once I became familiar with the practice, I found it to be most comforting, and eventually a preferred way of entering the sort of peaceful contemplation I had always longed for. Most recently my daily praying of the rosary is accompanied by a beautiful sense of Mary's mothering presence.

I, Mary Neill, began to say the rosary daily as part of the community prayer life when I entered the Dominican Order, which has a very special devotion to spreading its use. I always wanted the sound to be perfect, and was annoyed that some nuns prayed faster or slower, seemingly oblivious of the common pace. I remember the excitement of receiving a long fifteen-decade rosary to wear from my belt when I was first clothed in the religious habit. I remember learning to make and repair rosary beads (because I was always breaking mine, catching it on knobs and furniture.) My mother still has a beautiful moonstone rosary I made for her when I was a novice, thirty years ago.

The sense of the rosary as an inner work came in my late twenties, when I made a series of rosary novenas for certain goals which were important to me at that time. I received a strong response to my petitions, almost frightening in the change it brought to my life and relationships, and I remember being convinced that this way of repetitious praying did change my consciousness.

As the changes came after Vatican II, choral recitation of the rosary became optional, as did the wearing of the rosary — changes that were painful for some sisters. I did not find these changes hard, but I did keep the rosary by my bedside or under my pillow, to say, or just to finger. I went through a period when it was hard to identify with Mary as Mother (since I was resisting a lot of maternalistic structures, perhaps) but I trust the rosary as a tool even for the Aquarian Age because it engages all the functions — sensation, thought, feeling, intuition.

I recall being struck by Gurdjieff's comment to Katherine Hulme (noted in her autobiography), when she showed him the rosary. "Ah, it is a Mother thing." I have come to believe that the more consciously we relate to archetypes such as Mother, Father, Woman, Virgin, the less likely we are to fall unconsciously into a negative relationship to what the image means. For instance, if a woman who has not born children does not consciously acknowledge her need to be mother to someone or something, she may be overmothering and overbearing in an irritating or even dangerous way, because the impulse is disowned.

Writing this book is for me an effort to reanimate my devotion to Mary, to the beauty of the image of the rose, often seen as a symbol of the full blossoming of love, as in Dante's image of the white rose in Paradise.

✝ Part One

THE MYSTERIES OF MARY

The Mystery of Annunciation
Living with Surprise

In the sixth month the angel Gabriel was sent from God to a city of Galilee named Nazareth, to a virgin betrothed to a man whose name was Joseph, of the house of David; and the virgin's name was Mary. And he came to her and said, "Hail, O favored one, the Lord is with you!" But she was greatly troubled at the saying, and considered in her mind what sort of greeting this might be. And the angel said to her, "Do not be afraid, Mary, for you have found favor with God. And behold, you will conceive in your womb and bear a son, and you shall call his name Jesus.

He will be great, and will be called the Son
   of the Most High;
and the Lord God will give to him the throne
   of his father David,
and he will reign over the house of Jacob forever;
and of his kingdom there will be no end."

And Mary said to the angel, "How can this be, since I have no husband?"

And the angel said to her,

"The Holy Spirit will come upon you,
and the power of the Most High will overshadow you;
therefore the child to be born will be called holy,
the Son of God.

And behold, your kinswoman Elizabeth in her old age has also conceived a son; and this is the sixth month with her who

was called barren. For with God nothing will be impossible."
And Mary said, "Behold I am the handmaid of the Lord; let
it be to me according to your word." And the angel departed
from her.   (Luke 1:26–38)

Meditation on the Annunciation

BY RONDA CHERVIN

✝ I am Mary. As a child I loved the freshness of God's world — to
see the lilies of the field, the stars.... I pondered and pondered — why are the older ones so unhappy. Why are they so busy
clutching what they have and raging about what they do not have
with no time to love the gifts?

No one understood my thoughts except my cousin Elizabeth. I
loved to visit her. And one man in the village, Joseph. He too was
different.

It was good to listen to the holy books being read. They explained: the creation, the catastrophes, then the hope. I like to go
to the synagogue, where all the hate and fear in our people turns to
yearning hope. The Messiah will come . . . someday . . . sooner if
we pray harder and turn to Yahweh by pondering His way and doing His will.

When all the laboring is done and our house is asleep, I lie
awake, lifting up my heart to the heart of God, waiting, waiting,
waiting, for I know not what.

If I, Ronda, were telling the story of the annunciation as a
legend, I would have the Holy Spirit tell the angel Gabriel: "Go
find me a bride among the daughters of Adam!" Gabriel would
reply: "How shall I know her? There are millions of daughters of
Adam." The Holy Spirit would answer: "Fly over the villages of
men. The girl I seek has a pure heart seeking only what is from me.
She will draw you like a lodestar."

Carved into an infinite number of your statues, Mary, are your

14

fragile hands opened in receptivity and yearning for that which nothing but infinite love can fill.

As a man is drawn to a woman by the passionate openness of her yearning for him, so I imagine God's attraction to the woman He created to be the bride of His Spirit. Grace is God's love filling our openness. Mary was so full of grace that there was nothing to prevent His coming to her.

Elizabeth Barrett Browning wrote: "God's gifts put man's best dreams to shame." What was the highest Mary could dream? To be the mother of the Messiah, not the mother of God, the bride of His Spirit.

The future is the mother of surprise. For the fatalist, the past is the only mother and her children all look alike. For the Christian, every moment holds the promise of uniqueness as God ever reveals the new. The virgin soil in each of us must be open to the gift of the new seeds of life.

Mary, the recipient of the most splendid gift of honor and love offered to man by God, you become Our Lady of Surprise as the glorious Virgin of the apparitions at Guadalupe, Fatima, Lourdes.... You sweep into our lives out of the future to lift us who are mired too long in the mudpond of mundane concerns, or of degradation. But just when the ecstatic taste of heaven threatens to turn us into spiritual gluttons, lolling insensibly in the eternal, you, the resourceful mother, guardian of hearth and harvest, you shoo us back into the world to our tests.

Surprise is not the last step in confronting the annunciation. Mary is surprised, but then surrenders: "Be it done to me according to thy will."

Mary, you surrendered immediately to God's challenge because of your boundless trust in the Father of the future. I surrender only reluctantly with painful doubt to the unknown, clutching to myself, regretfully, the old unfulfilled dreams, as I step hesitently into the future, thereby slowing down my ultimate arrival at the place destined by God for me.

Kierkegaard claims that the self God has prophesied for us is our real personality. How consoling that no matter how I kick and scream in protest, the prophecy of God for me, as for the wise, trusting Mother of God, will someday come to pass, and all my prayers, my ponderings of His mysteries, will be answered and accomplished day by day, no matter what. "Be it done to me according to thy will."

How beautiful openness, surprise, and surrender sound. And yet I fear the new and refuse its mystery over and over again. I prefer to dwell snugly in dismal repetitions of sterile patterns rather than risk the new. To the hopeful, life is the bridegroom bearing gifts. To the fearful, life is a rapist.

I can go backwards into my past to see why the word surprise brings more dread than delight:

Surprise! your father is gone.
Surprise! your grandmother is dead.
Surprise! your grandfather is dead.
Surprise! *he* chose another woman.
Surprise! you are growing old.

Our Lady of Surprise, however, calls us out of our immersion in the disappointments of the past and beyond the shrewdness of the streetwise, to listen to the songs of eternity, the lullabies of Mary:

I am your Mother Mary.
Bring me along, little daughter.
Do not castrate the living God in frigid fear.
Let His angel come to open your clenched hands.
See, the gaze of the angel strips you
  of the rags of disillusion.
Only an open womb can receive new life.
When the darkness overwhelms you, bury your head
  in my lap.
Even sad surprises can be blessed.
From the crucifixion comes the resurrection.

16

Pain is deep, but joy is eternal.
Hail daughter, full of grace.
The Lord is with you, blessed are you among women.

Our Lady of Surprise teaches us to respond to change, to move beyond rigid sterile images. The Holy Spirit is the bridegroom coming with fresh visions for your future. Listen to him, let him espouse you to bring forth something new into the world. Perhaps it is a different approach to the same old tasks. Even terrible surprises are important in one's life tale. Even that which is so destructive to our smoothly established routines and plans shows us that there is a living God who initiates the dance, and that we are not spinning on a carousel alone.

Nevertheless, you will never mother the next phase of your life's tale unless you are first a free open maiden again drawing the Spirit to you by the passion of your yearning for Him; bringing rain or sunshine, His will be done.

Meditation on the Annunciation

BY MARY NEILL

Mary, small town Mary, whose relatives say with pride: "Well, she's marrying a man from David's House, you know, *King* David." How webbed you are in that small Nazareth; how tightly held in that small world full of old cousins (Elizabeth) and old stories (Father Jacob's dream of great posterity). How did you find the strength to stammer yes to all that luminous knocking to enter the small room of your body?

You knew enough to be afraid of the fine words of praise and promise, of this smooth stranger telling you of heights and kings and ancient promises of never-ending kingdoms. Everything is limited and you know it. So you say your protest: "I am a virgin; how can this be?" What did your words mean but to protest that you felt small and closed, far from heroes like David and Jacob.

So you wonder: "How can I, so emptied of life, be called to bring forth a strange new life that will divide my life in two—all lives in two—for all time? How can barrenness bring forth emptiness?"

And the answer comes to you: Barrenness has bloomed in your cousin Elizabeth, as it had in your ancient ancestresses Sarah and Phanuel. Yes, love comes only in the wilderness that arouses longing for life.

"Fiat," you say. "Let it be. . . ." And you welcome new life intruding upon yours.

Mary, when strangers call me to open my depth to them—to new relationships, to a new me, to life—I am shattered by earthquake and volcano. The containment of my old identity is threatened. For my kingdom is not that of David who wept for his sins nor of Jacob who struggled with an angel, but a fragile, illusory fortress, impervious to the assualts of pain, spewing forth, when embattled, much fire and stone and smoke, but showing few signs of life during the lull between battles.

How differently, Mary, you and I stand before the intrusions of the Lord that call on us to open ourselves to life in, with, and for others in love. Our hands are lifted in surprise, but while I scream, "No more intrusions, Lord!", you utter wonderingly but firmly, "Come in and let your will be done!" How can you, how can you?

And sometimes I do not even want you to teach me how you can. Antiseptic virgin, at seventeen, I closed my heart and womb from life. I offered it, I told myself, to God as I thought you did, but really not as you did. For I did so to avoid children who first tear apart one's womb and then at one's heartstrings, and a husband to whom I could offer only fortress walls and missiles.

But thirty years later, I now want the holy laughter of Sarah when she heard that her barrenness would bloom in Isaac (whose name means laughter), the holy laughter that comes only from softness freely given to intrusion. Can you help me, Mary? Is it too late for a stone maiden to conceive laughter, to say yes and yes again to life and to all its intrusions that destroy and yet create? In saying yes, yes, to the impossible, in loving and believing in a God for whom all things are possible, you, Mary, hold the key to the depths of my heart, so that I may say with you:

> I believe. Be it done to me according to your will.
> Take away my armour, Lord.
> Strengthen in me, Lord, the faith and hope that even in the most barren space and tightly enclosed worlds I will be inspired to seek, and be granted visions of, You in your glory.
> Teach me to discern and heed the voices that say,
> "You are full of grace — take life into you."
> Oh, Mary, teach me not to be afraid of life, of you, frail virgin, star of life's storm-tossed sea!

The Mystery of the Visitation
Giving and Receiving Support

In those days Mary arose and went with haste into the hill country, to a city of Judah, and she entered the house of Zechariah and greeted Elizabeth. And when Elizabeth heard the greeting of Mary, the babe leaped in her womb; and Elizabeth was filled with the Holy Spirit and she exclaimed with a loud cry, "Blessed are you among women, and blessed is the fruit of your womb! And why is this granted me that the mother of my Lord should come to me? For behold, when the voice of your greeting came to my ears, the babe in my womb leaped for joy. And blessed is she who believed that there would be a fulfillment of what was spoken to her from the Lord." And Mary said,

> "My soul magnifies the Lord,
> and my spirit rejoices in God my Savior,
> for he has regarded the low estate of his handmaiden.
> For behold, henceforth all generations will call me
>   blessed;
> for he who is mighty has done great things for me,
> and holy is his name.
> And his mercy is on those who fear him
>   from generation to generation.
> He has shown strength with his arm,
> he has scattered the proud in the imagination
>   of their hearts,
> he has put down the mighty from their thrones,

and exalted those of low degree;
he has filled the hungry with good things
and the rich he has sent empty away.
He has helped his servant Israel,
in remembrance of his mercy
as he spoke to our fathers,
to Abraham and to his posterity forever."

And Mary remained with her about three months, and
returned to her home. (Luke 1:39-56)

Meditation on Visitation

BY RONDA CHERVIN

† At first I held the mystery of the annunciation in my heart,
sealed in silence. Only when I was alone at night did I sing the
words of the angel to myself, to the babe, and to my God: "I am the
Bride of God, the Bride of God. . . . I will bring forth the Messiah,
the long awaited one who is growing inside me. Alleluia, alleluia,
alleluia!"

Who can I tell? Not my father and mother, not yet. They are
true servants of God, but shy away from the strangeness of His
ways, preferring to follow His Holy Writ, than to ask and ponder. I
will have to tell them soon, of course, and they will believe, but not
yet. I don't want to see their brows furrow or to feel their fear for
me. I want to exult in my joy . . . and Joseph, beautiful Joseph, but
not yet.

Elizabeth! Yes. Elizabeth, far now, but always near in spirit. She
will confirm me. When I was little I loved her most of all of my relatives. She taught me how to confirm. I asked her why other people always nag and scold though it does no good. Yet she always
saw the good in people and told them what was pleasing in them.
She put in words what I sensed, that inside everyone, even the most
gnarled countenance, was a beautiful dove. The words addressed
to others were a song at whose notes the dove inside would awaken
and flutter its wings and begin to fly. We played a little game

21

together. She would anoint someone with words of confirmation and I would smile as soon as I could see the dove in the shine of gratitude in their eyes or the sweetness of a little gesture.

Now it is I who need the confirmation. The holy dove has descended upon me but is still hidden within. She will confirm me and the lightness in my heart will fly out into the world. She, the bearer of another mystery, will know. Rejoicing together, we will banish the demon of dread that comes to me sometimes at night when I think of the shame that my wonderful secret must cause those who love me.

The mystery of the visitation can be seen as an icon of friendship. The philosopher Von Hildebrand taught me that all friendships are based on the values two persons appreciate in common. For instance, I feel friendly toward other women who knit. We can talk about the good feeling of the wool passing through our fingers and the joy of giving handmade afghans, sweaters, booties to those we love.

The more of me I can share, the more themes for the confirming friendship. Deeper friendships arise when we can commune in the loves that we carry deep within us. There is a special thrill when people meet who love the same leader. For hours they can talk about the way that beloved, admired person transformed their lives. Then how much further can the friendships go when they are based on sharing God, the apex of all beauty, goodness, truth, and love!?

But the confirming element of friendship includes even more than loving the same things. There is also a delight in the uniqueness of the other, and this pleasure makes the loved friend more beautiful, bringing out his hidden loveliness.

The true friend sees more in us than we see. We belittle ourselves so terribly. Mary knew she was bride of the Spirit, mother of the Son of the most High, but it is Elizabeth who calls her by that magnificent title, Mother of God, and then Mary's joy cannot be contained. It flows out in ecstatic themes which only the most glorious music of the great composers can contain. Have you heard the trumpet blasts triumphantly proclaiming Mary's Magnificat as Bach composed it? The first time I heard it was when I was still an atheist in a record store. Though I dwelt in the valley of darkness my heart leapt, and I bought it and played it at home over and over again, racing about the room in surging hope that my mind could not justify and my heart could not contain.

Meditation on the Visitation

BY MARY NEILL

Mary, I love that you rush to see Elizabeth — that you need to have the angel's silence broken for response to the hidden Word growing within you, who presses you to rush to the hill country. Up, up you go! And neither the darkness of the valleys from which you are coming nor the caves and tombs that lie ahead daunt you. It is hill-country time and the going is not steep.

I see you skipping over the hills, glad to be alive, glad to feel life within you, maybe singing from the Song of Songs: "My beloved comes skipping over the hills; arise my love, my dove. . . . Arise, my love, my dove, my beautiful one. . . . The voice of the turtle dove is heard in our land."

When you see Elizabeth, and four hearts leap for joy, your voices flash out your deepest thoughts, pondered long in silence. The words clarion the sign of the new dispensation — joy: "My heart praises. . . . My soul rejoices. . . . People will call me blessed!"

You are not afraid to be happy, to share that happiness and to sing it out. And what gives you the strength to be happy? For even mighty Augustine knew that being joyful requires a strong heart: "I was quite certain of these truths, but I was too weak to enjoy You," he writes.

It is not because confusion and mystery have ceased — that you are certain of your identity and role or that of your child. But you are certain about God: you know He is Savior; that He remembers;

that He does great things; that His name is holy; that He is almighty; that He reverses what the world does, exalting the lowly, humbling the proud; that He keeps promises; that He remembers to show mercy.

And how do you know so much for certain about God? Because you are like him. *You* show mercy—you rush to Elizabeth, confirming her—and letting yourself be confirmed. You share your word, as God shared His. You reveal yourself, and scatter any pride in your heart by owning that He is the potter, you, the clay. You remember the promises to Abraham, so you came to help the servant Israel, that is your aging cousin Elizabeth. You stretch out your strong young arm, not to magnificent kings, but lowly cousins. Elizabeth is right in marvelling aloud when she sees you: "Happy of all women and happy the son in your womb."

God comes to others because *you* come to others, bearing His love and tidings in your person and action. You do not wait, passive and confused at God's intrusion into your life. You hasten to be God's hands and voices to others. You know that God lives and does mighty deeds because you do mighty deeds. You have an excess of strength, you are certain of God's will for you. Any pain of isolation has ceased because God shows his love and confirmation of you through Elizabeth.

O Mary, teach me to be strong and certain, for when life bursts forth in and on me, I whine and clutch my few coins, afraid to pay the price of glory. I have not the strength. Life will devour me and spit me out. I guard against the robbers of my few coins, wise like Judas against extravagant Magdalenes.

I hide in my house with both my good news and bad—no skipping about the hill country to visit old women. The poor, the old, the sick—they remind me too much of my own inner poverty and weakness. The God of my fretful complaints is a weak God who neither punishes nor exalts. I am a hollow woman and my God is hollow, the J. Alfred Prufrock of the universe—no wonder it runs so badly! no wonder it seems not to run anywhere.

Mary, you run, you skip, you sing, you play, you share, you remember, you help, you laugh—and so does your God. Blessed

24

are you indeed, and blessed the God who imagined a woman like you.

So bless me Mary (for never was it known that anyone who fled to your protection, implored your help, or sought your intercession, was left unaided).

Give me your strength, your mighty arm, to break the idol of my weak and negligent God who never laughs or skips or plays or longed to flesh himself inside your flesh.

Give me the courage to bear the Word, to share my word, and to shatter the bonds of isolation that I have forged in fear against all kin and cousin.

Give me the strength to enjoy God, to be happy and to let it show, so that I can bear to hear the exclamation: Happy are you among women!

The Mystery of the Nativity
Creating the New

In those days a decree when out from Caesar Augustus that all the world should be enrolled. This was the first enrollment, when Quirinius was governor of Syria. And all went to be enrolled, each to his own city. And Joseph also went up from Galilee, from the city of Nazareth, to Judea, to the city of David, which is called Bethlehem, because he was of the house and lineage of David, to be enrolled with Mary, his betrothed, who was with child. And while they were there, the time came for her to be delivered. And she gave birth to her first-born son and wrapped him in swaddling cloths, and laid him in a manger, because there was no place for them in the inn.

And in that region there were shepherds out in the field, keeping watch over their flock by night. And an angel of the Lord appeared to them, and the glory of the Lord shone around them, and they were filled with fear. And the angel said to them, "Be not afraid; for behold, I bring you good news of a great joy which will come to all the people; for to you is born this day in the city of David a Savior, who is Christ the Lord. And this will be a sign for you: you will find a babe wrapped in swaddling cloths and lying in a manger." And suddenly there was with the angel a multitude of the heavenly host praising God and saying,
"Glory to God in the highest,
and on earth peace among men
with whom he is pleased!"

When the angels went away from them into heaven, the shepherds said to one another, "Let us go over to Bethlehem and see this thing that has happened, which the Lord has made known to us." And they went with haste, and found Mary and Joseph, and the babe lying in a manger. And when they saw it they made known the saying which had been told them concerning this child; and all who heard it wondered at what the shepherds told them. But Mary kept all these things, pondering them in her heart. And the shepherds returned, glorifying and praising God for all they had heard and seen, as it had been told them.   (Luke 2:1-20)

Meditation on the Nativity

BY RONDA CHERVIN

† I am Mary, heavy with the child who is to be the Savior. I had to come with Joseph. Do you understand? Full of grace though I am, still I am a woman, vulnerable, needing his strength for my protection and for the fathering of the child. And he needs me now. He needs to grow in the mystery we are carrying together as we move along our journey. Ever since his dream he becomes happier and happier in his undreamt-of role. He, himself, is astounded to see how the Spirit can turn uncertainty and sacrifice into holy faith and generosity.

But, of course, he is worried. I grow bigger and bigger and more and more tired. We must reach Bethlehem, the city of the census, but also of the prophecy. He would like to be able to picture the house of the baby's birth. So would I. I want to have walls around me within which to lie down and finally be done with the pain of the baby pressing to come out, and of the unsettling movements of the donkey over the bumpy roads.

Yet amidst the exhaustion there is the joy. Was following God's will ever easy? Not since Paradise and maybe not even then. But my son is the Promised One who will make the road easier, who will usher in the kingdom that will have no end. As we jog along I picture the kingdom, the heavenly Jerusalem. The words of the psalms sing in my heart and sometimes we sing them together as we proceed up and down the roads.

I am arriving in Bethlehem half dead. Joseph is searching for a place. The baby is descending. I grasp Joseph's hand and mutter prayers of surrender. I know my sufferings are so little for such a great joy.

Now I am being lowered onto the straw. Soon, soon, soon. Help, dear Joseph!

Sing, Joseph, sing Alleluia to the Lord! I whisper, for I cannot speak. He is wrapping Him in the beautiful garments mother Anna embroidered for my son. Light floods my heart. Mine. God's. The Son of David. The saviour of our people, Israel.

Who is coming in? Shepherds. They say the angels sent them. Of course. It does not amaze me that the angel Gabriel who came to Zachariah, me, and Joseph should come to announce the coming to the poor. What astounds me is that they, the shepherds, who I know to be the most doubting of men, should have believed. Now they are kneeling to him! Of course, the light is not just in my heart, but flooding the whole manger.

I am falling asleep now. The baby is sucking at my breast. Joseph sleeps by my side. The inmost is now without. I see Him and He sees me. All is grace.

G.K. Chesterton in *The Everlasting Man* claims that no tale in any religion can ever rival in beauty and awe the image of God as an infant in a manger. Yet that same paradoxical mystery also offends the intellect. How can the eternal God really enter time to be swaddled in diapers? Kierkegaard demanded to know. How can the omnipotent one be mere infant, the Spirit of the cosmos, a morsel of flesh? What holy revelation is to be witnessed at a birthing and in the presence of the newborn infant?

Last year, I witnessed the nativity in the form of a woman in labor whose childbirth I was allowed to watch. My friend, Elasah Drogin, was to have a delivery at the home of her midwife and close friend, Ann Govan, a fulltime nurse in a maternity ward.

To be honest, I was not eager to come and witness the event. My own childbearings were far from idyllic. In spite of all the instructions of natural childbirth experts, I shrieked through my short labors. Might not my friend Elasah, a tense type like me, also react as I had done? Thus I hoped that the call inviting me to the home delivery would find me out of the house.

But as Providence would have it, I was home when the call came. What I witnessed at that delivery will probably be the closest I will ever get to knowing what Mary's birthing of Christ was like. Elasah, in her travail, taught me what it means to suffer as a Christian, in a state of grace, penitentially.

With each contraction, Elasah's face remained undistorted but her eyes became deeper and deeper, more accepting of the penance of childbearing. None of my furious rebellion! She knew that pain is the price of life and she would pay it to the full.

Surrounding her, we sang and prayed aloud. Could Joseph of the chanting Jewish people have done less? Why do we imagine that he felt out of place and fussed with the animals instead of being intimately involved in this terrible but exquisite moment?

Then, came the last push. Under the patient guidance of the midwife's hands, the little baby's head came sliding out. Miraculously, there he was: Peter Nicholas Drogin!

Meditation on the Nativity

BY MARY NEILL

I read your Christmas story, Mary, that first fragile Christmas, and I am amazed that you could, in your single heart, contain so many opposites: Divine Emperor Augustus/new born child; northern Galilee/southern Bethlehem; King David/Carpenter Joseph; coming to your hometown/no room in the Inn; shepherds/kings; *armies* of angels/singing peace; open fields with flocks/cave with solitary manger. No wonder that you "remembered all these things and thought deeply about them" (Luke 2:16).

Brave heart to brave these contradictions and hold fast in love to God, husband, and child. No wonder we crown you with a contradictory title, virgin-mother.

This is census time, the first countdown of the "Divine" Augustus, and you leave home to go to Bethlehem, the house of Bread — your husband's hometown — as you count down the days until your son/sun arrives, who will lead all mankind back home.

The Beatles mournfully sang: "Once there was a way to get back homeward — once there was a way. Boy, you gotta carry that weight a long time." And so we have carried the weight of exile for a long time, believing that "you can never go home again." But swift heart, you knew better.

Home-girl Mary, who left home to make a home-away-from-home for Joseph. You, who could make a cave a home for God, can do the same in any and all desolate places. You are a portable home, the ark of the covenant, carrying the numinous presence wherever you walk. The shepherds, with eyes keen from night-watching (for surely only nightwatchmen who are caretakers see God's glory), were told that when they saw you and the baby and Joseph, they would find proof of the good news which would bring joy to all the people. So they hurried off and found Mary and Joseph and saw the baby in the manger. What they saw amazed them and sent them back singing praises to God.

Just what did they see? A poor couple, pressed to travel long and hard out of due season? Indigents with no influence and money for an inn? No cradle for their baby? No midwife? In this squalor they found the glory of God that caused them to sing? Yes, because all that was the frame, but not the picture. The picture was of a home; that was it, a home. A man and woman loving deeply amid profound limitations, cherishing life, bringing it forth in the cold of winter to the warmth of their love.

Surely Jesus' first clothing from you is this seamless garment of parental love that guarded his heart and flesh from birth to death. No dicing soldiers would steal this tunic. Where did he learn love but from your eyes and Joseph's? Where did he learn not to be afraid of death and loss? Where learn that God was his "Abba," but from his abba Joseph? Frail earthern trinity—mother, father, child—that shadows forth the Trinity of the highest heavens.

I envy you your Joseph with his skilled hands and patient heart who makes shepherds feel at home and does not turn his back to angel stories and women's birthing mysteries. Strong man who brought you forth as wife and mother, as you brought forth God as babe and Savior.

O Mother Mary, teach me to be a home, have a home, but do not let me be content to cling to my abode in the land of exile in which I dwell with comforts. Teach me to find my home as an orphan and stranger among orphans and strangers. Teach me not to fear the journey, I who always make sure that I have reservations at an inn with clean sheets (cow dung and sheep out of sight!) whenever I do venture forth from home; I who would despise the aid of a rough carpenter or the praise of silly shepherds—I turn to the people who "count":—and do not count myself among the huddled masses who get counted by the Divine Augustuses.

O Seat of Wisdom, I ask you:
Help me not to be afraid of angel voices singing praise,
- of dark birthing caves and of the poverty within them;
- of rough helping hands;
- of clashing opposites within and without myself;
- of mother love that weaves a seamless garment of comfort from womb to tomb;
- of carrying Jesus wherever I go;
- of being a home to myself and for others.
You refuge of sinners, ark of the covenant, seat of wisdom!

The Mystery of the Presentation
Handing on the Tradition

And when the time came for their purification according to
the law of Moses, they brought him up to Jerusalem to present him to the Lord (as it is written in the law of the Lord,
"Every male that opens the womb shall be called holy to the
Lord") and to offer a sacrifice according to what is said in the
law of the Lord, "a pair of turtledoves, or two young pigeons."
Now there was a man in Jerusalem, whose name was Simeon,
and this man was righteous and devout, looking for the con-
solation of Israel, and the Holy Spirit was upon him. And it
had been revealed to him by the Holy Spirit that he should
not see death before he had seen the Lord's Christ. And in-
spired by the Spirit he came into the temple; and when the
parents brought in the child Jesus, to do for him according to
the custom of the law, he took him up in his arms and blessed
God and said,

"Lord, now lettest thou thy servant depart in peace,
according to thy word;
for mine eyes have seen thy salvation
which thou hast prepared in the presence
   of all peoples,
a light for revelation to the Gentiles,
and for glory to thy people Israel."

And his father and his mother marveled at what was said
about him; and Simeon blessed them and said to Mary his
mother,

> *"Behold, this child is set for the fall*
> *and rising of many in Israel,*
> *and for a sign that is spoken against*
> *(and a sword will pierce through your own soul also),*
> *that thoughts out of many hearts may be revealed."*

And there was a prophetess, Anna, the daughter of Phanuel, of the tribe of Asher; she was of a great age, having lived with her husband seven years from her virginity, and as a widow till she was eighty-four. She did not depart from the temple, worshiping with fasting and prayer night and day. And coming up at that very hour she gave thanks to God, and spoke of him to all who were looking for the redemption of Jerusalem.

And when they had performed everything according to the law of the Lord, they returned into Galilee, to their own city, Nazareth. And the child grew and became strong, filled with wisdom; and the favor of God was upon him. (Luke 2:22–40)

Meditation on the Presentation

BY RONDA CHERVIN

✝ I am Mary, a Jewish woman. I remember the excitement of all new mothers taking their firstborn son to the temple, blending pride with the mystical knowledge that this child belongs to God. The child is being taken from the narrow confines of the mother's embrace and offered to Yahweh in heaven, then carried home, blessed by ancient ritual. He belongs to God, community, and family at once.

And now it is my turn, my heart swelling with exultation, for my son is not only the son of my flesh, family and community, but the Son of God, begotten of the Holy Spirit, the long-awaited one, the promise, and I am His mother. It is our secret, Joseph's and mine, as we take Him triumphantly to the temple. When the women come to coo over us, to say how much He looks like me or Joseph, we sing in our hearts how much He will look like the Holy Spirit. We have seen the Shekinah Glory shining in Him. We who longed night and day for the Light now live with the Light moment by moment before our eyes, in our arms. Just a little moment of pain, my Jesus, when you are circumcized. It is nothing. Do you know that my Jesus. Pain is but a moment in the eternity of joy which is your Father's heart. Yes, you know. I look into your luminous eyes and know that you know.

Look, they are coming! The old saints, Simeon and Anna. They are coming to salute you, my darling. Of course they know you. Rejoice Jerusalem, your Savior is here!

Our era seems to witness some groups moving away from external manifestations and celebration and others moving towards them. Many Christians have become alienated from Church rites and want to live their faith as a private, even hidden, orientation. Others seek the comfort of ritual, moving from loose cultural settings to highly structured ones.

I come from an untraditional background in which religious rituals were mocked as superstitious and hypocritical, and which made family celebrations as informal as possible. In becoming a Catholic, it was the not the rituals which attracted me at all, but rather the substance of the belief that Christ was really personally in the sacraments. Only gradually did I come to understand the motherly function of regular celebrations in rooting the spirit securely in the good earth of the kingdom.

I also came to regard refusal of the public exhibition of one's faith in community as a form of pride. One imagines that one's own faith is pristine, not to be sullied by the deficiencies of others. In reality, it is the support of the community of believers through their prayers and sacrifices that has nurtured the individual throughout the centuries. The same is true in family life. At times of proud aloofness, one imagines that one does not need the others. In reality, qualities in others, missing in oneself, are what give one strength. The defects of group unity are so visible, yet the bonds of this unity are so much stronger and profound.

Meditation on the Presentation

BY MARY NEILL

And now Mary, you make another journey—up, up, higher now to Jerusalem, up to the temple whose destruction your son will prophecy and effect. He will be convicted, perhaps not entirely guiltless, on the charge that he swore to destroy the temple.

So many journeys you have been on and will further make, walking with Joseph for a while, as now, helping with the baby, buying doves. Then walking with Jesus who will soon be gone, and then with strangers, until you walk no more. "What ways, heart, you have been, what sights you saw and will more now in longer lights' delay" (Gerard Manley Hopkins).

So short the bliss. Already the shattering of tranquility begins; you begin now to purchase the purification from smooth illusions. First and last, whatever the price, you willingly pay—whether two doves, a sharp sword through the heart, or an empty tomb. "My ways are not your ways," Yahweh revealed. We mortals flee separation, loss, decay, but they are all part of His ways of love, and you experienced and endured and embraced the full truth of that love. Did He teach you slowly, as He has me, or were you a fast learner? How early on did you learn that light shines only against the darkness?

Simeon holds the child high now, a small eucharist in aged arms, and sees the light the shepherds saw. "With my eyes I have seen your salvation." He sees too the light flowing from this body that will destroy as well as save; a word which will contradict many people, revealing their secret thoughts. What does that mean— their secret thoughts? What are *your* secret thoughts as you stand amazed?

"Led by the Spirit" Simeon was "covered by the Spirit" as you were. Who is the ghostly bridegroom—the word that conceives life? Who gives words to Simeon and Anna, those ancient temple birds whose longing keeps them close to the great walls? Were you fright-

35

ened of the longing in yourself and in others, suddenly whipped by those ghostly winds of the Spirit, or had you learned to dance in whatever direction they whirled your life?

You, and Joseph too, are the doves sacrificed—your peace sacrificed to the fire and sword that your son will cast upon the earth and into your hearts. "And sorrow, like a sharp sword, will pierce your heart." And did you say, "just so—I always knew it." when you heard these words? Or did you understand and remember them only later when you stood at Calvary looking at your son's pierced side?

Mary, this I know and honor you in knowing: the Church, His bride, was created from out of His sleeping body, drawn forth from His open side with the love flowing from His pierced heart. And that pierced heart of His with its infinite love was created and sustained by you and your heart, ever pierced again and again for His sake. Only broken hearts can love with the love that conquers hell; all other loves are fluff upon the wind. Jesus, the babe, broke forth from your womb; Christ emerged from your broken heart. Your womb and heart, beseiged and scaled by God; you build the temple of the heavenly Jerusalem while Simeon and Anna, ancient doves, coo over the baby from Nazareth in the earthly Jerusalem.

Why is this a joyful mystery, Mary? Simeon's joy? Anna's joy? Tell me how to feel the joy that comes from words that comfort not, from words that are true, but not kind to hear. Teach me, Mary, to purify my illusions and love the truth that renews the earth, destroying and creating.

I do not like the feel of wounded hearts. When I was a broken woman, I hid it well under wit and charm, and danced the dance of a thousands veils. Nobody wants to have or see a wounded heart. And who cares for comfort from old codgers in the church/temple who long and pray and fast and long and pray and fast? What do they get as a gift? Only a couple too poor to buy a sheep? What have you lived for but to see a baby doomed to die too soon because He won't keep His Word shut up. What a religious system! Couldn't you, after Simeon's warning, have trained that child better to not cross authority, and to not heed the wind that led Him in the desert?

The son you exchanged for doves was a volcano, pushing from the heart of the earth, through the sea of seas into the heart of the world, pouring out lava/life that burned and flowed before it cooled into earth that would generate flowers and trees. Where did you get the strength to live near a volcano?

So help me, Mary of the doves:
- to find joy in the joy of others, as you did with Anna and Simeon;
- not to be afraid of going up and up to my Jerusalem where my illusions of omnipotence will be purified;
- to love the law of life which the Mosaic Law only dimly foreshadowed: that the Lord takes as He gives, and gives as He takes;
- not to hate my wounded heart, but to ever find the broken Christ amidst its shards;
- to learn to dance with the ghostly Bridegroom who lives in my deepest longings and knows the secret thoughts that I fear to think;
- to love and let go; to love and let;
- to love the volcanic me.

The Mystery of the Finding in the Temple : *Losing and Keeping*

Now his parents went to Jerusalem every year at the feast of the Passover. And when he was twelve years old, they went up according to custom; and when the feast was ended, as they were returning, the boy Jesus stayed behind in Jerusalem. His parents did not know it, but supposing him to be in the company they went a day's journey, and they sought him among their kinsfolk and acquaintances; and when they did not find him, they returned to Jerusalem, seeking him. After three days they found him in the temple, sitting among the teachers, listening to them and asking them questions; and all who heard him were amazed at his understanding and his answers. And when they saw him they were astonished; and his mother said to him, "Son, why have you treated us so? Behold, your father and I have been looking for you anxiously." And he said to them, "How is it that you sought me? Did you not know that I must be in my Father's house?" And they did not understand the saying which he spoke to them. And he went down with them and came to Nazareth, and was obedient to them; and his mother kept all these things in her heart.

And Jesus increased in wisdom and in stature, and in favor with God and man. (Luke 2:41–52)

Meditation on the Finding in the Temple

BY RONDA CHERVIN

✝ I am Mary, singing pilgrim songs on the road to Jerusalem. It is difficult to journey from our village — the endless preparations for the long trek — but once we are off, it is our joy to go with the crowds toward the Holy City. How much more so as each year my son grows in age and grace. My kinsmen, do they recognize who He is? I think not. A bit, yes. There is a certain reverence by them for His pure goodness. They never see Him do one of the many cruel things most boys do. The other children come to Him to judge their disputes and to invent games better than they ever could dream of. And he loves to laugh. On the rounds of my work I hear Him laughing with Joseph or the village men. Most of all, my heart bursts with pride to hear the wisdom of His thoughts. The best ones He keeps for me, for He knows I will treasure them in my heart.

Now we are trudging back from Jerusalem, sad at departing, but happy to see our city teeming with people coming from so far to praise the Holy One.

Where is my Jesus? I told Him we would be leaving. He always does what He knows is necessary. He will be meandering among the kinsmen telling and hearing stories of Jerusalem. "Joseph, where is Jesus?" "I have not see Him yet!" Fear, anger, more fear, terror, my feet growing swifter and swifter as I seek Him futilely on the road. Did he wander off into the hills to pray, as He does so often in Nazareth, in His need to escape the swarming village, to be alone with His Father?

Finally His face. We have not lost Him. There He is. How princely He sits among the elders. How they hang on His words. Jesus! Why did not You tell us? How could we know?

I am ashamed and confused. He wanted me to have known not by His words but by prayer that He had to remain behind. What does that mean? No. His hour has not yet come. I know that. I am

39

His mother. Oh, He does know it too. He is coming with us after all.

As we trudge along toward Nazareth, my Jesus is quieter than usual. I wonder if He will feel confined in our village.?

Did I not always know He was for all of Israel and not just for us — or did I? He knows He is not to be a carpenter for life. But I, His mother, know how much He needs us still. His dream, is it not to make all of the earth a home of God, as heaven is for man and God. Is it not from the home of our hearts, mine and Joseph's, that He will draw His homespun images? How I love to hear the stories He tells in the streets to the children about the ways of Yahweh.

I take his hand and smile. He smiles too and all is well.

This mystery challenges us to accept the pains of comings and goings. Sometimes we refuse to leave the nest of home's security, a secure job, tradition, etc. . . . We want to be the child in the womb rather than the mother or father ourselves. We refuse to grow. Is the image of growth so popular in our times because it is so contrary to our innermost fears?

Sometimes we refuse the homecoming. Always wanderers, job-hoppers, dilettantes, rebels, we avoid commitment and roots.

But the Church calls us into the home of her beautiful sanctuaries, her history, her community of saints and sinners, past and present and future, to be nourished and then sent out to do the will of the Father.

Another facet of the mystery of journeying and homecoming is the balance between the unusual and the ordinary. Quiet people often prefer the ordinary to the volcanic eruptions of the unexpected, the stimulating. These people are the homebodies who have to be forced out by extraordinary and inescapable crises. Then there are the fiery spirits for whom the ordinary seems mediocre and unbearably tedious. Being forced into stable, repetitive patterns is to them deadly.

Seeing splendor in the ordinary and peace in the midst of storm is the gift of wholeness to be found in truly holy people. Mary and

Jesus represent to our spirits both a consciousness able to delight in the mundane and routine, and the visionary yearning, the courage and trust of the pilgrim and crusader on the most perilous spiritual journeys ever made: Mary, who assumed the terrible but glorious burden of being Mother to God and His first and greatest disciple; Jesus, who battled Satan, undercutting proud error with homespun parables, and forgiving betrayal, contempt, and murder with the loving peace of the Father.

The mystery of the Finding in the Temple has often been probed for symbols of the journey that parents must make in gradually releasing their growing children to adult independence. We parents must slowly loosen our hold on our children, substituting lighter cords of mutual respect for chains of possessive authority. In struggling with the intense desire to protect my teenagers against the world and their own darker urges, I turned to the older women of my parish who have already made this stage of the journey. They all say the same to me: love and let go, love and let go. Because you cannot control them does not mean God cannot protect and save them.

Meditation on the Finding in the Temple

BY MARY NEILL

Mary, I let myself feel your panic in this mystery. Where is my child? Why was I not more careful? How did I lose Him? What will the relatives think? Why didn't He tell me where He was going?

You look for Him in the group. He is not there. You look for Him in the streets—He is so easy to find in Nazareth—so hard to find here. You call His name—no answer. Only the worry in Joseph's eyes stems your panic. "Why did we come here with this mob for the Passover?" you think. You call and look and call and look. He, that warm and loving presence who has followed your footsteps for twelve years now, twelve perfect years, is gone. He is lost. You are lost. A great Passover is taking place within you and within Him. When you find Him at last, you see Him as though through Red Sea water—distant He sits with teachers in the Temple listening and asking questions. You are amazed and they are amazed.

All the answers He found in you have pushed him out and away. He is now teaching by his very listening, by his questioning and by his answers. You were His teacher and now He teaches the teachers; now He teaches you.

I feel the anxiety and loss and anger rising in you as you ask, "Why have you done this?" I imagine your secret thoughts: "Why have you passed from child to man, from town to city, from listening to teaching, from found to lost, all at once, without warning? You never told me, prepared me. You are leaving us, leaving me. It isn't fair. Flesh of my flesh, bone of my bone. So like me, and now you are so strange to me. You are lost to me, and I am lost in looking for you. Will I always be looking for you from now on? Tracking you through strange streets? Is this what my saying "yes" twelve years ago implied—my willingness to let myself be lost for love of God. To receive His gift and then to lose it all? Must I search the house all night for a small coin? Must I now seek all my life for my one small child, now lost?

And then the child answers you: "Why did you have to look for me? Did you not know that I had to be in my Father's house?"

You do not understand. The book so says but I imagine that in part you did. Perhaps you did not understand that this passover foreshadows the greater passover to come—the journey to Jerusalem from which He will not return. But you understood something of the Father's house. For you have taught Him to call God Father.

You taught Him of the promise and protection of the temple—of the Shekinah. You sang to Him the songs of Yahweh who saves, who is the rock, the fortress, the firmament, whose name is holy. You showed him the sparrows and said not one of them fell without Yahweh's loving Providence. You touched His hair and said His Abba, heavenly Father, had each one counted. You showed Him the lilies of the field and rehearsed their names with Him and said that not Solomon in all his glory was clothed as these were. He watched you bake bread and you told Him that He could not live by bread alone.

You told him stories of Solomon and Sheba, David and the Ark, of Noah, Lot and his wife, Elizabeth and the widow of Sarepthah. He watched you patching His and Joseph's clothes and learned that no one puts new patches on old clothes; nor new wine in old wineskins, you added, and you let Him sip the wine. He saw that you were poor and sometime hungry, that you wept and had been rejected. And he knew that your happiness in God, in Him, and in Joseph was a strong bulwark against these hurts.

Any kingdom that He would ever rule would be buttressed by such paradoxical joy and enduring love. "Blessed are the peacemakers for they are pure of heart." He would come to say this because He had first seen their blessedness in you. And when He would be temped to fight for the kinds of kingdoms desired by men of pomp and circumstance where no king washed his servants' feet, He remembered the hands that washed His feet, the heart that steadied His vision, and He chose a kingdom that first He touched at your side and saw in your eyes again and again.

You taught Him all the words for what He saw: figs, houses built on rock, children piping in the market place, prostitutes and tax collectors, lamps on lampstands, foxes in dens, birds in nests, lambs and wolves, oxen and donkeys, borrowed loaves of bread, scorpions and eggs, snakes, purses, sandals, moth, rust, rainclouds, south winds, bushels of flour and batches of dough, hens and chicks, salt that lost its savor, pigs and goats, prodigal sons, olive oil for food and fuel, dogs and lepers, millstones, vineyards, slaves, and tenants. And so when He taught of His kingdom, He used these homely words that He learned at your side, rather than the scholars' words He had heard at twelve when He was found by you in the temple amid the doctors.

And so your joy is great that what you had lost to strangers and strangeness now is found again, and you sense your restfulness with these rhythms of your life — the waxing and waning, the fullness, the emptiness of your body and heart. And now the lostness and the finding. You will always know how to find Him now. So your joy no one can take from you. The small triangle of your family will explode upon the world and its bursting will inflame the world. And your joy is great that you first banked those fires and warmed that hearth where the light of the world came to love the world in so much concrete splendor. "I, if I be lifted up, shall draw all things to me," He can say because you have lifted Him up, drawn Him to you, and given Him away to the world, "knowing that you will get Him back a hundredfold." How happy He is to go back down, now to Nazareth, and obey you and His Joseph, to be contained again in your love which makes a home of this hard world.

O, Mary, home-maker, home-mother, teach me to cherish lostness, for:

- I hate losing those I love;
- I hate the panic of "What did I do wrong?"
- I hate my pleading, "Why didn't you tell me?"
- I hate strangeness where once I felt familiarity;
- I like fancy abstractions and philosophical prose.

So I pray, help me to embrace my lostness, knowing I will be found by God's maternal love with which He clothed you. Help me not to be afraid of Jesus, for I can see that you too were somewhat afraid of this strange child. I find Him familiar, yet over there, against me somehow. I see that you must have felt the strangeness I feel; and yet you held out your arms to Him in welcoming love.

- Help me love the Jesus who stands over and against me, demanding that I search for Him in the city streets.
- Help me love the Jesus who makes me angry, whom I cannot find in a crowd, who does not tell me what He is doing, who has a plan I am not entirely in on, and who expects that I will know all about the Father's house just because I live in it.
- Give me your Joseph who stands silent while you talk and name, fret and blame.
- Take me down to Nazareth with you and teach me to obey the law of life and love.

The Mystery of the Agony
in the Garden : *Crying Out*

And he came out, and went, as was his custom, to the Mount of Olives; and the disciples followed him. And when he came to the place he said to them, "Pray that you may not enter into temptation." And he withdrew from them about a stone's throw, and knelt down and prayed, "Father, if thou art willing, remove this cup from me; nevertheless not my will, but thine, be done." And there appeared to him an angel from heaven, strengthening him. And being in an agony he prayed more earnestly; and his sweat became like great drops of blood falling down upon the ground. And when he rose from prayer, he came to the disciples and found them sleeping for sorrow, and he said to them, "Why do you sleep? Rise and pray that you may not enter into temptation."(Luke 22:39–46)

Meditation on the Agony in the Garden

BY RONDA CHERVIN

I know, Jesus, that in your Gethsemane night, all of *our* sins flooded your consciousness. You knew with devastating clarity what we were and what we could do to you for ages to come, and you wept, even in blood. Your realizations, at that very moment, were being confirmed by your betrayal by your friend Judas, and your sleeping friends' neglect. Yet you came forth not hating, but forgiving. What dearly consoling words these are: "Forgive them for they know not what they do."

And during your Gethsemane, dear Jesus, did you think of your mother's face, the way it always looked when she saw neighbors victimized by the cruelty of others? I picture her enveloping the victim in her compassion, yet piercing the sinner with a gaze of infinite sadness: Poor you! Don't you know of the Father's love for the both of you? Holy Mary, mother of God, pray for us sinners, now and at the hour of our Agony, amen.

In the hour of agony, we try to close up the doors of our hearts, grit our teeth, clench our fists, and tighten our lips, that undaunted by internal bleeding, our life may go on as usual. After all, why drown in the quicksand of emotion. Tears cannot help. Better to harden our hearts and let work and time and tranquilizers cure all, than to "trouble deaf heavens with our bootless cries."

Yet I shudder at the nauseating night revelations! It is the time of Satan's possession, but long does he go unrecognized by me. Instead, all the evil thoughts I have flooding my mind about the people I encountered during the day—about deadly motives behind their every word and act—appear to me to be established truth. Yes, and not only that, but who am I to condemn, for am I not deserving of their calumny and persecution, miserable wretch that I am? And no one exists to save me or them. Nothing is salvageable for any of us. So why not kill myself!

I hastily rise in the night, go to the bathroom, then splash my face and hands as if for purification—may all this inner filth disappear! Back to bed. My husband groggily asks: "Are you okay, honey?" I quickly mutter, "Yes, I'm fine. Go back to sleep." Let my husband stay asleep lest his Gethsemane song join mine to tear my heart to pieces even more.

At times like this, only reaching for the Mother, the rosary of Mary under my pillow, can bring a measure of peace.

Crying out implies trust that someone is listening, even from afar. In our worst agonies it seems that no one near or far can hear, and, yet, we still cry out.

> *There is no God, the foolish saith.*
> *But none, "There is no sorrow."*
> *And nature oft the cry of faith*
> *In bitter need will borrow.*
>
> Elizabeth Barret Browning

In the throes of pain we beg like Jesus that the cup be taken away. And if the chalice is not taken away, we have three options: flight, fight, or surrender.

Peter chose to fight, then flee. John chose to flee, but finally surrendered beneath the Cross. Jesus chose to surrender: "Thy will be done, be done, be done . . ."

Oh, Lady of Sorrow, collect our tears in the chalice of atonement. Help us to cry with pain lest we cry instead only with rage. Bring us to our Saviour that our blood may mingle with His, that we may whisper in the night: "Father, *my* Father, if You will let this chalice pass . . . but not my will, Thine be done." Holy Mary, mother of God, pray for us sinners now and at the hour of our agony.

Meditation on the Agony in the Garden

BY MARY NEILL

Oh Jesus, I drag myself to this garden scene, the reversal of that other garden, Eden, where Adam had declared: "I will not serve. I will walk where I will and eat what I desire." Where upon opening his eyes after he had sinned, seeing that he was naked and separate, he betrayed his wife. Where rather than calling on God, God had to call to him: "Where are you Adam?" God had to ask.

Jesus, new Adam, God never had to ask You where You were,

for You never left off calling Him: "Stay with me, look at me, comfort me. You who are now over and against me. I tread the olive press for You. I am crushed with sorrow, the blood and sweat not sweet wine, my tears and taste are a searing salt."

And where are you, Mary-mother, where is your comforting presence? Did you hear about the garden scene afterwards—from His betrayer Peter? Utterly alone He was, separated from the sleeping sheep whom He had faithfully tended and guarded, healing, feeding, comforting, and warning them. Yet they could not give Him even one hour, one word. They did not stay awake to see the new Adam creating love from chaos and betrayal. They left Him utterly alone on the margin of the world.

And you, new Eve, are utterly alone, far from Him. You who would never betray Him, whose flesh was willing and spirit strong—you were not there. He who entrusted Himself and His Way to you now entrusts His life to the faltering disciples who, at best, will not even look at his need, and, at worst, even kiss Him unto His death.

I feel the pain of Your aloneness and Your betrayal, Jesus. You promised: "I will never leave you orphans." Yet You are left betrayed and alone to struggle with God, who will not leave You with just a shrunken sinew as He did with Jacob, but with all Your flesh and heart pierced to death. Your Father gives You over in that dark garden to the Prince of Darkness who has entered Judas' heart. *Never* did you ask *why?*

You say: "Take this cup away, Father, my Father." And even the angels could not look upon Your pain without rushing to comfort you. Your face touches the earth, downward to that dark mother You descend. Clay from clay, You hide Your face in surrender. Dark earth and all its darkest evil is Your only mother there. Still You cry and call into the darkness: Abba! You conquer the Prince of Darkness and the dark mother he rules by bowing down, by bending low, by calling out, and by flinging Yourself into that dark with only that thin fluted cry of Abba to save You from the pit. That is all there is—the cry. There is no face of Abba. You are no-face, no-name; you who are all men crushed to the earth,

48

betrayed by those who should have loved them best, and Your thunderous heart holds itself not tightly in self-pity and resentment, but breaks open and apart in love. It breaks to flood that garden, then the world.

Brave heart! No wonder that the disciples could not look upon that heart, but slept. No man can see the heart of God. How could mortal eyes see here the molding, churning, erupting creation of the Heart of Christ, and live?

I imagine Judas catching a mere glimpse of that great Heart and fleeing to money he could count and understand. For had he willed to be smelted in that cauldron Heart of Yours, what spendid alchemy would transubstantiate his soul! He could have, after that, stayed Judas Iscariot no more than Peter would stay Simon once he had drunk the cup of His Lord.

Oh Lord, You strengthen the weak by becoming one of them; You sift hearts by letting Yours be sifted. This moment, betrayed by friends, not enemies, just a stone's throw from help that never arrived — this was surely the nadir of Your life. Later, there will be no possibility of help, but here, for a moment, You could be comforted. Three times You wake your friends and ask them to watch. You are not ashamed to plead over and over again, as you later would thrice times ask Peter, "Do you love me?"

Yes, Lord, You need to know we love You; you are like us in all things save sin. And what does sin mean? Sin means not looking, not asking, lying, refusing, covering over with darkness, trusting the darkness. It means sleeping when the hour demands of us to be awake.

You faltered and fell, feeling a failure in Your inability to elicit enduring love and strength from those You loved; failing, too, in the strong protest of Your heart and body against the suffering Your Abba willed for You. Surely you must have hoped, before coming to the garden, when You pondered the inevitable suffering of the Son of Man, that You might be able to endure it without such shuddering fear!

Brave heart, brave man, brave Savior! Woe to those who come to this garden with You. You will sift them. They will fall and break, as Judas on the stone, or as Peter into a love so great that it will bind him and lead him where he would rather not go. Is that the way it always is? The deepest love that can cross the dark valleys of Cedron and be nearly crushed in the garden olive press; a love that stretches out on a high green hill for all to see — this love leads us, breaks us, stretches us, so that we go where we never imagined we would or could go?

It was hard for me to come to the garden with You Jesus; but now it is hard for me to leave. So I pray to You, in Augustine's words: "Oh Christ, for Your sacred name's sake, for Your bitter passion's sake, for Your infinite mercy's sake, forgive and forget what I have been, pity, oh pity, what I am: satisfy for what I deserve, and grant what I desire. Oh my Savior, You sought me when I fled from you. Will You reject me now that I seek You?"

Jesus! Help me not to be afraid of the dark gardens.

- Help me not to betray with a kiss.
- Help me not to hate those whom I counted on for help, who could not or would not share or even witness in compassion my suffering.
- Help me to trust the comforting angel who comes when no man hears my cry.
- Help me to kiss the earth when I would prefer to curse and rail against suffering that seems unjust.
- Help me to recognize my inner Judas who is too frightened to turn to Your heart and beg for forgiveness.
- Help me to know Abba whose dark face conquers all darkness that can assail my heart.

Oh ABBA! ABBA! ABBA!

The Scourging : *Enduring Violence*

So Pilate, wishing to satisfy the crowd, released for them
Barabbas; and having scourged Jesus, he delivered him to be
crucified.   (Mark 15:15)

Meditation on the Scourging

BY RONDA CHERVIN

✝ Rage! Red-hot, choking rage! Lava from the volcano of hate!
Release yourself!

I am Caiaphas, the High Priest. Strike, beat, batter; my words
scourge the blasphemous Nazarene. But when they fail to annihi-
late him, I rend my garments, baring my breast against his unyielding glance.

I am Pilate, the Roman procurator. I scourge with the superior-
ity of my skepticism. Like a father of squabbling children, I begin
to hate the victim as much as the victimizer for disturbing my
peace. Let them tear each other to shreds! Who am I to grapple
with their inexhaustible blasphemers?!

I am a Roman soldier, disgusted with the tedium of foreign ser-
vice in this miserable province. And here is this miserable wretch
before me, another one of those stubborn Jewish fanatics who pro-

longs the length and discomfort of my exile here. To the devil with you and your people, and with unsettling silence and submission — damned Jewish pride and resistance in another mask, huh? I'll have my men rip it all to shreds, Nazarene!

I am Jesus of Nazareth. With their misunderstanding and rejection, my people flay my spirit and flesh so dreadfully. Father, Father! Give me strength to love them until the end. Through sheets of sweat and blood I see the pitifully shrunken souls of my persecutors. And those of all the violent people to come, from age to age, world without end. Father, forgive them, for they know not what they do.

Violence is everywhere condemned, yet flourishes everywhere. I flagellate those who are weaker while I do not dare to strike the stronger. I make scapegoats of the victims who have no protection and escape from my abuse: family members, fellow-workers, absent bosses. Moreover, I lacerate the shortcomings in myself that I find absolutely intolerable. "Of all beasts the man-beast is the worst: to others and himself, the cruellest foe," wrote Richard Baxter in the seventeenth century.

At times, my violence is outright and crude: I yell and scream and hit. But more often it is invisible and subtle, yet no less deadly effective. "And hated with the gall of gentle souls," wrote the lady of the sweet sonnets, Elizabeth B. Browning.

But there are also positive images of violence. Flannery O'Conner entitled a book with a seldom quoted phrase from the gospels, "The kingdom of heaven suffereth violence and the violent bear it away." "I have come to bring not peace but a sword," proclaimed our gentle Savior. Patrick White, the Australian Nobel-Prize-winning novelist, envisions God as the great vivisectionist, tearing open His creatures, pain being the miracle truth serum that He offers to save man from his disgusting complacency.

Violent is the righteous anger of the Lord scourging the money changers in the Temple. Violent is His sarcastic refutation of the sophistries of the leaders who ridiculed and rejected His message. Violent is the Lord when He refuses our urgent appeals for unending happiness, slamming the door on our most fervent desires. Violent is His insistent demand that we crucify our hatred rather than our enemy. Violent is the Lord who tears us away from our cozy life-style and quiet prayers to look upon and respond with the eyes and heart of Jesus to our fellow man as the person of Jesus incarnated for us. And violent must be our efforts to fulfill this demand by transforming ourselves and our world into His person and kingdom. Many are the ways from which a person can flee from scourging. One may cringe so low that the whip misses one. One may flatter so well that the whip never falls. One may carry such a swift and brutal whip oneself that no one dare attack. How terrifying and disturbing are the phrases of Jesus insisting that those who follow Him will and must suffer while those well-loved by men who are spared scourging in this life will suffer in eternity.

Meditation on the Scourging

BY MARY NEILL

O Lord Jesus, king of hearts in that dark garden, surviving bloody betrayal and agonized sweat with bitter-free heart, now I see you become the ace of sorrows, clinging to the pillar — hard stone bride that keeps you from falling. Your body is whipped and racked, kneaded and torn: softened for its final dissolution and transformation into the Bread of Life that will leaven the world.

They are trying to beat shame into you, shame for walking outside the grooved tracts of society, for drawing crowds, for talking too much, for making riddles, for *being* a riddle. And the power which flowed from your body is now beaten down and away so that they look upon you as the "One despised and the most abject of men, whereupon we esteem him not."

God the Father, who showed His face in your eyes, your face, your hands, and your strong body, is beaten down inward. Smaller and smaller the divine light implodes until only you know it darkly in the thin litany that never fails to be in your heart: Abba. Abba, your heart beats, Abba, Abba. Slow, then fast, as the soldiers beat your back and sides.

The more quietly and deeply you move within, the emptier you become, the more the soldiers try to beat you down, to beat out your secret, to make you resist and curse. Your passivity inflames them and they make fire in your body like the agonizing blaze that seared and sealed your heart in the garden.

This body, carried by Mary, perfumed by the Magdalen, warmed by John's head resting on your heart, and kissed by friend and betrayer, is being prepared for the wedding feast — the marriage on the high hill that will consummate the union of all opposites. Sin and forgiveness, submission and action, God and man, north and south, east and west, city and countryside, virgin and prostitute, Roman Law and the New Law: all opposites will collide and explode in you. You will open your heart and flesh and pour out, you strangely feminine Bridegroom, receiving and opening as much as penetrating and spilling out.

What a contrast to the preparations for earthly nuptials. The bride and bridegroom anoint their bodies and cover them with fine garments readying themselves for gentle caressing of flesh and hearts. Eros comes to their dark wedding chamber to intoxicate and comfort. You, Lord, have been often to such wedding preparations and feasts, teasing, I'm sure, the wedding couple in their awkwardness and beauty. Where did you learn, strange Bridegroom, to reverse the order of Eros and flagellation for your heavenly marriage?

So many earthly marriages begin with caresses and erotic transport, but end in mutual flagellation, cruel scourgings for lost dreams and daily jabs that corrode the spirit. The sado-masochists we read about who use leather and chains are not alien beings whose nature and life-style bear no semblance to our own, but rather, they offer focused and clear symbols of where so many "normal" intimate relations end — in mutual degradation and battering. Pornography sells because its symbols unveil a dark corner of the human heart. The sado-masochism such literature portrays is motivated by the reasoning that, if I beat you, I feel alive because life moves and cringes under my hand, and if I let you beat me, at least I have a physical focus for my pain, so I know where I hurt and why. But does not such desparate hunger for a sense of being alive and master of life, and diffused spiritual pain that achingly demands to be pinned down to some identifiable and conquerable source, to some degree characterize all people, especially in their efforts to use relationships to fulfill these needs?

Jesus, I know that you hate this mutilation of your body and that you are sickened by this absurdity. Yet you do not whine and do not look into your persecutors' eyes and turn them to stone. You cover their sins from your sight with an abundance of love, as you just turned Peter's frozen, frightened heart into a blaze of penitent-grateful love with one fire-love glance. You love to love and be loved, and yet you go bravely to the unyielding stone pillar-bride. You do not turn from this rape and rack of love reversed from the order in which the world knows love.

O Jesus, forgive and forget what I have been and pity, oh, pity, what I am!

- For I easily lacerate with my tongue and scourge with my wit, protection against the absurdities and brutalities of life.
- For I despise the lacerations that always come with love, and dread the caresses as merely preparations for the scourgings to come.
- For my heart winces when former students come back and show in their eyes their beatenness. Life has battered them in ten years time. What will it do to them at fifty? What then will their eyes show?
- For I read of children, infants even, who are brutally abused by their parents and wonder why you do not exempt little children from your passion. No one, to you it seems, is too small, too frail, and too beautiful to be exempted from the cruel, unmothering world.
- For I became a nun, a spouse of Christ, to flee from the flames of Eros, with their earthquake-ecstasies and traumas, only to find you unwilling to leave these flames of Eros banked against the world, myself, and you. Eros leads to God, St. Augustine said. I thought I could leap past the flames to God, but I have merely flung myself into the conflagration time and time again.

55

So you sought me when I fled from you; will you reject me now that I seek you?

Help me to seek deeper faith that God uses Eros by reversing the order of caresses and scourging. Let me take my beatings with free will and focused mind. Put down my hand that seeks revenge and moves to reverse the spiritual order of growth: that "Love first takes something from you before it gives."

- Help me to guard against a sado-masochism in my being that attempts to live the truth of life's suffering through degraded and non-life-giving symbols.
- Help me to love my body, so often beaten by my own neglect, and to keep it open to feeling and life. Let me become a woman unafraid of desire that exists to be transformed in the cauldron of your love.
- Help me not to be afraid of taking action towards consummating my inner marriage as you did, even in your courageous passivity as you watched your beloved Abba diminish into a tight ball in a small corner of your heart, sustained only by the ragged beat of your suffering heart, suffering the mockery and brutality of uncomprehending, rejecting man.

The Mystery of the Crowning
with Thorns : *Accepting Humiliation*

> And the soldiers led him away inside the palace (that is, the
> praetorium); and they called together the whole battalion.
> And they clothed him in a purple cloak, and plaiting a crown
> of thorns they put it on him. And they began to salute him,
> "Hail, King of the Jews!" And they struck his head with a
> reed, and spat upon him, and they knelt down in homage to
> him. And when they had mocked him, they stripped him of
> the purple cloak, and put his own clothes on him. And they
> led him out to crucify him.   (Mark 15:16-20)

Meditation on the Crowning with Thorns

BY RONDA CHERVIN

✝ Jesus, I imagine these as your thoughts: In a delirium of pain
there come a few moments of oblivion to savor sensations from the
past: my mother's soft embrace, the scent of Mary Magdalen's per-
fume still in my hair, the warm head of John leaning on my breast
—the faces of those who have loved me like roses opening before
my delighted gaze.

I open my eyes to see soldiers approaching me again. Their
grimacing faces dance wildly as my vision careens, until one of

them brings forth a hideous crown, not of roses, but of thorns, and smashes it down on my head. Raucously they jeer, "Hail, King of the Jews!" Father! thy will be done! I am a lamb led to the slaughter.

An insidious and familiar voice whispers in my ear, "Destroy them! You fool, summon the angelic hosts. In one instant they will be gone. You will be free to go where people will give you what you deserve, Son of God!" Depart from me! I cry. Get thee behind me Satan!

Father, this is love, to lay down my life for my friends. Again that voice: "Friends? What friends? THESE?!"

Yes, Father, forgive them. For they know not what they do!

In his book *Fear and Trembling*, Sören Kierkegaard shows how one passes from being a Knight of Resignation to becoming a Knight of Faith. Most Christians never make even the first difficult yet crucial step. Using Abraham as his model, Kierkegaard showed how necessary it was for that patriarch to renounce all possibility of saving his only son before his hope could become authentic. With infinite resignation, the believer must put all things into the hands of God and be ready to sacrifice every earthly good should that be the will of a God who is far above all rational understanding. Then having given all into God's hands, Abraham became a Knight of Faith by daring to hope that this same God would answer the prayer of his heart.

Jesus in His passion is the model for such seemingly irrational perfect trust in the Father. How logical it would be for Jesus to say: "That's enough. I will suffer the agony, and I will even allow myself to be scourged. But to be ridiculed in *your* name, dear Father, is too much!" But Jesus, perfect Son of the Father, let Himself become total victim with unconditional resignation.

How differently we Christians approach the crown of suffering. We say: "I didn't deserve this. That was bad enough, but this is too much to be endured! No one can expect anyone to forgive this!" Human reasoning asserts: " Is it not natural and God-given for man to wish for just rewards? Does not Jesus Himself promise that the good will be rewarded?"

For instance, it is hard for mothers to resign themselves to the ingratitude of offspring. The mother gives and gives. But the children first take her for granted, then reject her, and finally fling her gifts back to her, often with words of mockery and bitterness: "I didn't ask to be born. Who are you to tell me anything, you who . . . .! It's a free country! I hope I never become like you!"

It seems that only when mothers — parents in general — renounce all hope of grateful love does such love begin to manifest itself in offspring. First parents must understand that children "know not what they do," and forgive from the heart. The father of the Prodigal Son first lets the ingrate son leave with his inheritance, knowing the son will squander it all. Then, having resigned himself to never seeing that beloved one again, hope begins to grow. Each day before sunset the father walks to the hill where he can see from afar whether his son might be returning. Because the father's heart is not in stoic negation, he is ready with wine and fatted calf for his son's converted heart.

Some move from sadness to resignation to hope. But most often people go from the feeling of being mistreated to bitterness, then to retaliation. "Revenge is sweet," as the saying goes. I must admit to having cherished grievances for decades about injustices of a few minutes duration.

I watch myself when I become bitchy, when I fight dirty, and when my heart is full of hostility, and I ask when this ill-feeling all started? Usually there is no satisfactory answer. Could just one quickly spoken word trigger such hatred in me? No, the cause of such anger lies in deeper wounds whose painful surfaces those few words have grazed. The crowning with thorns may have taken place long ago, but the immediate situation served to push one of the thorns in some inches deeper.

Spiritual exercises in the healing of memory are helping many people to find the point in the past where the hurts took place.

Back in the place of greatest pain, the Christian is to imagine the face of Jesus crowned with thorns. From this vision, we learn to take comfort, accept our own pain, be cleansed of bitterness, forgive, and hope for reconciliation.

Very often a certain amount of psychological counseling is helpful or necessary. We need to make the journey into our moments of shameful self-hatred or bitterness toward others in the company of an experienced traveler.

Meditation on the Crowning with Thorns

BY MARY NEILL

Jesus, your heart was broken in the garden, your back and side flayed at the pillar, and now your head is crowned with thorns, as bored and cynical soldiers make you their pastime toy, their game. "You wanna be a king, huh!? All right, we'll make you king! Hey, we're kneeling before you! C'mon, we'll even let you prophesy! You are Blindman's Bluff, we've bluffed you; now, guess who we are? Who are we, you rabble-rouser Jew?"

"Yes, and who are you, Jesus, to think you can stir the coils of power against you and not be strangled in those coils? You fool, you clown. Where are your friends now? The crowds who cried, 'Hosanna! Be our king!' The fools who hung on your every word and clung to your garments?"

"You king of fools! the soldiers cry. Here, take this purple robe and this 'kingly' crown and be our king as we laugh and spit on you. We make you our Red Rover, and we cry 'Come over; come over.' Why don't you look at us? Why don't you break down under our blows? What are you thinking?"

Jesus, I wonder, too: what are your secret thoughts? What keeps you so still and centered and so far away from them even as they move in and press harder upon you? Or is it just that you are too racked to think at all? Are the thoughts themselves worse than the thorns that tear your head?

60

I once thought that you had a beatific-vision sort of parachute that protected you from the suffering of confusion, doubt, and squalor of swirling images and thoughts which my mind can thrust upon me, the conflicting notions and multiple images that can make my mind a vortex of muddied water. But I now believe that you experienced fully the mental, emotional, and physical suffering to which you were so brutally exposed. Immersed in your pain, the throbbing head and back and broken heart beat a steady rhythm: Abba, Abba, forgive them, forgive them.

Were the thorns a gift to keep you from thinking? I fail before the power of your mind and heart—vast enough to encompass this scene containing all the anguish of the ages, and yet not go mad. For it can be comforting to go mad, Jesus; to shield oneself behind that umbrella of psychological misery which preserves one from the real misery of life. You did not go mad. You, powerful King of Light and Love, who facing disgruntled soldiers, faltering apostles, and even the Prince of Darkness, stood strong in the face of all the opposition they could hurl at you.

All the complexities and nuances in you became one thought, thinking one thing, and one will, willing one thing: the purity of heart and mind that encircles all the vagrant inclinations and thoughts into one crown that does not pierce and rack the heart and mind. Is this the one thought: "I AND THE FATHER ARE ONE. And because we are one, I and these soldiers are one. I and these thorns are one; I and the crowds are one. I and life are one. All things come from the Father. All things sweet, sour, dim, bright, dappled. Lifted up, I will draw all things back to oneness in Him. Full circle."

This magic circling thought from the Father back to the Father joins Jesus, his heart beating "Abba," and the music of mind and heart echoes "Forgive them; for I am one with them." Jesus, the bridge over whom sinful man—brutal soldiers, harlots, tax collectors, virgins, priests—will walk to reach the Father. Jesus, lay down your life before them so that they may walk upon you. So far are their thoughts and ways from those of the Father that you must play the crazy clown dangling grotesquely in purple robes on the high hill, calling, "Come over, come over to me!" The pain is but a passage, the cruel thoughts a road to clarity, to join man's heart and mind to God's. The divided heart is a rude harp to sound the two notes: "Abba, I am Red Rover; come over, come over."

And so Christ, forgive and forget what I have been. Pity, oh pity what I am! For I am:

- Unwilling to think one thought and will one thing. Instead, I regard people who do as fanatical and always in trouble. I prefer to speak with a forked tongue and think a thousand veiled thoughts;
- Addicted to the fine strokes, obeisance, and compliments of the world. I walk like a queen, my friends say, and I demand equivalent treatment. I want to be queen everyday!
  - Fearful of the Father who is king of your wild heart. A "Father and fondler of hearts (he) has wrung," who in his dark descending is most merciful;
- Repelled by clowns, and you are king of clowns, of broken hearts and squalid life stories. Do not call me, I say, to your treacherous and tragic crownship-clownship. You who sought me when I fled from you, will you reject me now when I seek you?
- Help me to "come over, come over to you; Red Rover of hearts."
- Be my bridge over troubled thoughts and divided loyalties;
- Let me unveil my thoughts and circle them with the crown of your truth. Help me ring around about and out of my head my rosy illusions;
- Help me to "behold the man" that stood so pathetically and grotesquely before Pilate's soldiers;
- Help me to behold the God that stands before my door daily and keeps calling me and all nations to Him, over Him to the Father of all. "Our King comes in glory," the nations shout.

The Mystery of the Carrying
of the Cross : *Flowing with Pain*

And as they led him away, they seized one Simon of Cyrene, who was coming in from the country, and laid on him the cross, to carry it behind Jesus. And there followed him a great multitude of the people, and of women who bewailed and lamented him. But Jesus turning to them said, "Daughters of Jerusalem, do not weep for me, but weep for yourselves and for your children. For behold, the days are coming when they will say, 'Blessed are the barren, and the wombs that never bore, and the breasts that never gave suck!' Then they will begin to say to the mountains, 'Fall on us'; and to the hills, 'Cover us.' For if they do this when the wood is green, what will happen when it is dry?"   (Luke 23:26–31)

Meditation on the Carrying of the Cross

BY RONDA CHERVIN

✝ When I contemplate your carrying of the cross, Jesus, I hear Humanity's pain-river chant: No Father, that one is just too much for me. I am not strong enough, for the load is too heavy. You see, I am not like those other ones who carry this kind of burden. They are stronger. You, Jesus, — and Mary — become stronger from car-

63

rying the load. But I, well...I am too young, ignorant, scared . . . . And instead of looking strong and noble, the only times I have tried to take on a load, I came out of the effort in pieces, looking so ugly, nervous, stupid and bad!

All right, I'll give it a try. Oh, my God! See! I've fallen already under its massive weight. I told you I could not do it.

What? Someone's trying to wipe off my sweaty face! Who is it? A stranger; someone who cannot stay with me or know and understand me. So now it's even worse than before. A little comfort, and the burden seems worse afterwards!

Now someone's coming to help carry my load! Well, I'm not sure I want his help! Ugh! Fallen again! Well, I surely need the help, don't I?! I wish I could lie here forever! But I can't any longer. This burden is now mine forever.

I want to run away, straight into the crowds, and just disappear. Is the end of the road in sight? Each moment seems to me like a hundred years.

What? The burden suddenly seems lighter! It's been taken from me. My back is nearly broken! No wonder; I've reached the end of the road. It's a place of execution to which the road has brought me! And I can finally lay down my weary body and lie still — as they nail me to the burden that I've managed to carry so long, so far. I and it are henceforth forever one.

Many seek to disembark when the boat of life begins to be pulled into pain-river. How can we do this? We can jump overboard and abandon the ties that threaten to pull us into the vortex. Or we can sail on, lulled to sleep by drink or drugs. Or we can work so hard at rowing against the tide that we become too tired to fear and weep. At a certain level, all crosses borne for long periods of time are alike, whether they are the pain of sickness, loneliness, overwork, or whatever.

At first, the cross brings a sense that it is too heavy. Then, that this cross cannot be God's will because we are carrying it so clumsily. Instead of looking sanctified by the effort, we appear more demoralized and ludicrous each day we carry it. How desirable does it seem to be able to suffer glamorously, Hollywood-style! I prefer the vividly horrible paintings of the Passion, for only they can match my deepest feelings of humiliation and despair as I fall and fall and fall under the burden of the cross.

The impulse to flee from the cross is an ever-present temptation. But to flee from it, is to paradoxically become nailed to it, for the cross that is sent to us is our own, demanding that our body and spirit be shaped by and grow in the effort to carry it to its destination.

Once crushed by the weight of a cross and believing I would die of it, I heard a hymn about Jesus, and suddenly I wept upon learning that pain was not just a part of a life, but WAS life, WAS Jesus. Then I stretched out my arms and received my cross and my tears became a river that joined His, and I was ready to go on.

Francis Bacon wrote: "Prosperity is the blessing of the Old Testament. Adversity is the blessing of the New, which carrieth the greater benediction."

Meditation on the Carrying of the Cross

BY MARY NEILL

I leave the sight of your encircled head encircling my thoughts that want to stray, to fall asleep — anything other than to gaze upon the face of truth, so single and clear, as clear as your gaze which penetrates all deceit. I now hasten to the carrying of the cross where Veronica will imprint that face upon her veil and on her soul.

You are so tired now, Jesus. You stagger with fatigue and emptiness. Everything is pierced now: heart, flesh, head. What more can be pulled from this empty form? You are the hollowed out man being limned out by the authorities, the crowds, your disciples, and your Father. Rich you strode the streets of Nazareth and Galilee, swiftly you whipped with strong arm the money changers. Poor now, without your followers, you stagger, and your arms struggle to hold the cross beam.

But this is really better now than in the garden where no hands helped you. Here, Simon of Cyrene bears the cross for a while; Veronica wipes your sweat: the women mourn, and your mother's eyes look for one still moment into yours with a love and anguish so profound that you can gather strength to make that last hard mile.

Long-distance runner, Jesus. This is the last lap, and you care not whether you stumble and fall, again and again and again. You will make it to the high hill; you will break open the skull of death on that skull calvary.

There is so little space in these narrow streets for you who loved the desert and the open fields; no space to think, to feel, and to be alone. The crowd, which you knew early on was not to be trusted ("for you knew what was in the hearts of men"), presses too close, eager to see the hero of this parade. With all the noise and confusion, can you even hear the heart that still insistently beats, Abba!?

"If in the green wood they do these things, what will be done in the dry?" you ask the women of Jerusalem. Curious words of comfort for them and for you. You are green wood, the new tree of life to be planted on the hill of Calvary. The tree of life hanging from a tree. Carpenter with his cross beam hammering a new creation, and being hammered upon at the cross points of the world. Stretched to the north, south, east, and west, you draw all things to you.

But now you drag, now drop, now fall, now fumble. The lamb is on a narrow wooden bed led to the slaughter, gives himself over to the wolf pack; lays down his life for the Lion, his Father. You are stripped now, clothes gone, friends gone, strength gone—all gone—and you are fastened to the cross.

You hold fast to the cross for those who would flee, for those who run from the truth, from death, from life. Walk no more; touch no more, you who walked the long walk and touched the dead to life. Now touch death; eat this bitter wood.

What did you see, Jesus, as you staggered on, so tired, longing for the cessation of pain? What were your secret thoughts? "I can go no more, not one step further! I won't get up. I won't look in my mother's eyes for the pain will be too great. I want to curse those

66

wailing women; I won't be stripped; I won't be pinned down! I won't; I won't; I won't; I want, I want. Abba. Abba. Abba.

"One step — Abba! Another step — Abba! Abba, all the way now. I can see the end coming. In me the Father is well pleased. In him I am well pleased. Abba suffers in me for those who cannot believe a God strong enough to create the world, could love a falling, failing creature made of clay. When I fall, Abba falls, for the Father and I are one. When one of my sheep falls, I too will fall, for I and my disciples are one.

"I am the bridge. I have talked the talk, now I walk the walk. And I say to all: See me, see the Father. See me fall and see the Father falling in love with His creation. Through me, fastened to the cross, see Abba fastening himself into the world's process of concrete splendor and its loss.

"The Father calls me to the high green hill and although my feet stumble, my spirit flies. I have longed to eat this Passover. I have longed to walk this last mile for the Father; to give my extra tunic to whoever asks; to turn my right cheek to him who strikes my left. This I learned from the Father, and now this I teach step by slow step, drop by bloody drop, nail by nail.

"Fastened, I am free. The Father's beams of love have placed this cross beam on my shoulder and I wear it as my yoke of glory. 'My yoke is easy and my burden is light,' I tell my sheep, and I do this because my Father's yoke IS light and easy. His love, a magnet, pulls me to the hill where I will give over to him and his creation that last gift left in me — my spirit, which now pushes me to that mound where my body will turn to cold stone, my blood to water. And my last breath, my spirit will pour out upon the world to catch it afire.

"Hurry, tired feet! Straighten tired shoulders! The consummation is in sight! 'Abba, Abba!'

"O Christ, forgive and forget what I have been, and pity, oh pity what I am," for:

- I cannot bear to fall again and again and show my weakness to others;

67

- I cannot gladly take the help when someone offers to help shoulder my burden;
- I ignore the comforting women always on the way to Calvary;
- I cannot be cabinned, cribbed, and confined by pressing crowds and hands;
- I will not be pinned down, fastened, stripped before my friends and foes;
- I will not be lifted up and regard my suffering as my hour of glory.

So, "you who sought me when I fled from you, will you reject me now when I seek you?"

- Help me know your Abba who willed for you the way of the cross and helped your every step;
- Help me know the freedom of being emptied out to become a vessel of God's grace and love;
- Help me be a long-distance runner like you who walked steadily up to the last mile, unafraid to trip and crawl as well as run and fly, in order to get to the end. Let me rejoice only in that I accept God's grace to move with God's grace to the finish!

The Mystery of the Crucifixion
Relating to the End

And they brought him to the place called Golgotha and they offered him wine mingled with myrrh; but he did not take it. And they crucified him, and divided his garments among them, casting lots for them, to decide what each should take. And it was the third hour, when they crucified him. And the inscription of the charge against him read, "The King of the Jews." And with him they crucified two robbers, one on his right and one on his left. And those who passed by derided him, wagging their heads, and saying, "Aha! You who would destroy the temple and build it in three days, save yourself and come down from the cross!" So also the chief priests mocked him to one another with the scribes, saying, "He saved others; he cannot save himself. Let the Christ, the King of Israel, come down now from the cross that we may see and believe."

And when the sixth hour had come, there was darkness over the whole land until the ninth hour. And at the ninth hour Jesus cried with a loud voice, "Eloi, Eloi, lama Sabachthani?" which means, "My God, my God, why hast thou forsaken me?" (Mark 15:22–34)

One of the criminals who were hanged railed at him, saying, "Are you not the Christ? Save yourself and us!" But the other rebuked him, saying, "Do you not fear God, since you are under the same sentence of condemnation? And we indeed justly; for we are receiving the due reward of our deeds; but this man has done nothing wrong." And he said, "Jesus, remember me when you come in your kingly power." And he said to him, "Truly, I say to you, today you will be with me in Paradise." (Luke 23:39-43)

So the soldiers did this; but standing by the cross of Jesus were his mother, and his mother's sister, Mary the wife of Clopas, and Mary Magdalene. When Jesus saw his mother, and the disciple whom he loved standing near, he said to his mother, "Woman, behold your son!" Then he said to the disciple, "Behold your mother!" And from that hour the disciple took her to his own home. (John 19:25-27)

And Jesus uttered a loud cry, and breathed his last.... And when the centurion, who stood facing him, saw that he thus breathed his last, he said, "Truly this man was a son of God!" (Mark 15:36-39)

But when they came to Jesus and saw that he was already dead, they did not break his legs. But one of the soldiers pierced his side with a spear, and at once there came out blood and water. (John 19:33-34)

Meditation on the Mystery of the Crucifixion

BY RONDA CHERVIN

✝ I am Mary, mother of Jesus.

Last time we met, I asked him, "Jesus, my son, shall we be together for the Passover?" He stared at me hard and said, "Yes, my mother." "And where shall it be so that you can join me?" "I do not know where it shall be yet. I will have it made known to you." Now it is Passover and I cannot find him. I know he is in Jerusalem somewhere but I am told he is hidden.

All through the ceremonies, dreadful images pass through my mind. They are cutting up the lamb at the table and I see my Jesus, like Isaac, being tied down for the sacrifice. I cannot sleep this night. At dawn I am pacing the house of my kinspeople. I wish Joseph were with me.

Now Mary, mother of Clopas, comes to tell me to make haste. We must go to him. She cannot bear to tell me, but I know where the road is leading. When Jesus and I used to pass near that hill on our pilgrimages, we would stop to pray for the miserable ones hanging on their crosses. Jesus would kiss their feet and wipe away the blood as I did.

My heart stops beating when I recognize his beloved form. He is naked. Where is the tunic without seam I made to cover him forever with my love?

No! The pain is too great for me to bear! My beloved only son. His gaze is searching mine. He wants me to share his agony, but not to give way. It is so important to him that together we make this moment a gift of love to the Father. I remember that he told me it must be this way, but I would not believe it.

My kinswoman and I take turns holding each other. I seem to be dead from agony, but still his words sink deep as they always have. "My God, my God, why hast thou forsaken me?" We always prayed the psalms together. I know he is thinking of the victory when it is over and this is what gives him courage.

The words of Simeon in the temple are flowing back to me. Your heart shall be pierced. Yes, it is true! For any mother what dagger is sharper than to see a child die before her eyes? "A light to the Gentiles, a glory to our people, Israel." I clutch the prophecies to my breast.

Just as I am wondering if I can bear it any longer, I hear Jesus proclaiming the salvation of the thief at his side. The glory of our people has come. The atonement is beginning. The gates of heaven are opening. The sky is darkening. Any moment will be the end of the world.

"Woman, behold thy son." He is calling me woman because I was all women to him, the new Eve, and mother of the Kingdom. He taught me to be mother to all, even to his beloved Mary Magdalen, now weeping at his feet, washing his feet with her tears again. I cannot comfort her now. She is engulfed in her pain, totally one with his pain. "Son, behold thy mother." Good John, the one closest to the hidden secrets of my son's heart, is holding me tighter. I love John. Surrounded by his strength I let myself sink into the pain.

I hear the voice of the centurion. Jesus taught me to love even the Romans. "Beneath that brutal armour lie tender hearts in need of the balm of your prayers," he told me. The centurion is saying, "Surely he was the son of God!"

Was! Was! It is consummated! Let me hold him at last. I will kiss his wounds and wash the blood off of his face with my tears. The son belongs again to his mother.

Afraid of death, the final one and all the lesser ones of rejection, loss, aging, etc., I tend to flee to a fantasy world where there are no crosses and paradise is free for nothing—or so it may appear.

At other times, I rail against my cross, screaming out anger and fear as I writhe on my cross like the other unredeemed thief beside Jesus.

"It's a weary world," runs another train of reasoning, like James Barrie's "and nobody bides in it." Why cling to a life in which, most of the time, one is forced to eat crow? Shake off your world-weariness and welcome death and resurrection. Only from the dark womb of death will new life come. But new life comes to us on earth through the cross. We ought not refuse the healing balm of confessing our sins, preferring instead to believe that the burden of guilt can be lifted by the shrug of a shoulder or a slippery excuse. Sometimes we accept the gift of forgiveness in our innermost hearts, but fail to make outward revelation of our guilt; and then our comfort is less. Ultimately, satisfying liberation from death and suffering can be found only in the cross, so that one can rejoice with the saints, "Oh happy fault which called forth such a Savior!" And in the end, death, too, is a mother holding us in her arms in our last agony, carrying us to the waiting embrace of the Father.

Meditation on the Crucifixion

BY MARY NEILL

Now, Jesus, you crown your life by dying. Fully conscious, fully relational, your heart and mind and body are open to all that Abba has willed for you.

When I have imagined my death, I picture those around calming me, loving me, telling me I count, helping dull the pain of separation and loss. Me, me—I am the center of my dying, and I would draw all energies and thoughts to myself. I would focus on my life, my death—and I would be afraid.

How differently you teach me to die, Jesus. You died so differently from all other men, that those who beheld your death would say, "Surely this was the Son of God." Those who preached you, first preached your death and resurrection—only later, your life, and much later, your birth.

You who are bridge to the Father reach out relentlessly in death to those who stand near—friend and foe alike. You relate to your enemies: "Father, forgive them." You are free not to hate them; instead you can look into them: you can look in their eyes, watch them dicing for your last worldly goods, and you can embrace them with compassion for their blindness and lostness—the small comfort they have in winning an extra tunic.

You relate, moreover, even to the criminals dying with you: "You shall be with me in Paradise," you say to one whose indignation for you buys him heaven. A man for others, you do not wait for comfort from your mother and your best friend. You rush to comfort them: "Mary, you shall be his mother; you, John, shall be her son." "Woman" you call her, full helpmeet to your suffering, vessel of your compassion and ceaseless will to relate. Naked of all worldly goods, still you give, marrying poverty and aloneness so that all who follow may learn access to the richness of a love that nothing can steal.

Fully conscious, you run neither from neighbor nor from yourself. You relate to the desolation of your soul; you do not hide its pain and anguish, its abandonment by the Father. "Why have you forsaken me?" you cry—powerful legacy to those who will feel far from God and yet can know in you their friend, like them in all things save sin, sin that is always essentially nonrelatedness.

The truth is that you are dying a hard death and you do not go gentle into that good night: a lamb, yes; but also a lion who can roar in desolation and cry in thirst in that wilderness. "I thirst," you cry and you relate to your own dear body's needs, the body that served you so well carrying you through dusty roads and deserts, hilltops, seashores, crowded streets. Ashamed neither of your dryness of spirit, nor the aridity of your body, you cry, "I thirst." "Give me to drink," you asked the woman at the well. And she gave.

No water comes here. Wine vinegar is given you by harsh men. Water has become bitter wine, and wine will become water and blood, and then blood will become water and wine. As your substance is poured out on the cross, all bodily and heavenly chemistries begin their strange reversals. When you are dead, others will name you God, as they never did when you were alive; broken, you will heal as never you did when strong and unbroken. All relationships shall change because of the way you related—excluding nothing and no one. "And I, if I be lifted up, shall draw all things to me."

Little wonder that you say, "It is finished." Consummated. The marriage of life and death has been consummated, and death does not win, nor does fleshy life, but a third thing is born from their union: a consciousness that can say Yes to life, knowing that death is its attendant; a consciousness that can say Yes to death, knowing that life is death's attendant. You taught us, Jesus, not to prefer life over death or death over life; not man over woman nor woman over man; not man over God. The lion lies down with the lamb; and God lays down his life and power in you that men may know that in their dying, they may lie down with God. Marriage Broker, Bridegroom, you marry death and bring forth life. From your sleeping side the Church is born, as Eve from Adam, and you give life to her that she may give life to men.

74

"And giving a loud cry, he gave up the spirit." You cry as in the travail of birth and *give*. No one takes your life from you; you give and give freely — pressed down, shaken out, and running over.

So, Jesus, I ask you to help me be a bridge; to stay conscious of my relatedness to myself, my friends and neighbors, my enemies.

- Help me not to separate life from death, but to know that they are sisters and live accordingly.
- Give me the courage to accept the abundance you have given me, and free me to give it open-handedly.

The Mystery of the
Resurrection : *Touching Again*

And when the sabbath was past, Mary Magdalene, and Mary
the mother of James, and Salome, bought spices, so that they
might go and anoint him. And very early on the first day of
the week they went to the tomb when the sun had risen. And
they were saying to one another, "Who will roll away the
stone for us from the door of the tomb?" And looking up,
they saw that the stone was rolled back; for it was very large.
And entering the tomb, they saw a young man sitting on the
right side, dressed in a white robe; and they were amazed.
And he said to them, "Do not be amazed; you seek Jesus of
Nazareth, who was crucified. He has risen, he is not here; see
the place where they laid him. But go, tell his disciples and
Peter that he is going before you to Galilee; there you will see
him, as he told you." And they went out and fled from the
tomb; for trembling and astonishment had come upon them;
and they said nothing to any one, for they were afraid.

(Mark 16:1–8)

Now on the first day of the week Mary Magdalene came to
the tomb early, while it was still dark, and saw that the stone
had been taken away from the tomb. So she ran, and went to
Simon Peter and the other disciple, the one whom Jesus
loved, and said to them, "They have taken the Lord out of
the tomb, and we do not know where they have laid him."
Peter then came out with the other disciple, and they went

toward the tomb. They both ran, but the other disciple out-ran Peter and reached the tomb first; and stooping to look in, he saw the linen cloths lying there, but he did not go in. Then Simon Peter came, following him, and he went into the tomb; he saw the linen cloths lying, and the napkin, which had been on his head, not lying with the linen cloths but rolled up in a place by itself. Then the other disciple, who reached the tomb first, also went in, and he saw and be-lieved; for as yet they did not know the scripture, that he must rise from the dead. Then the disciples went back to their homes.

But Mary stood weeping outside the tomb, and as she wept she stooped to look into the tomb; and she saw two angels in white, sitting where the body of Jesus had lain, one at the head and one at the feet. They said to her, "Woman, why are you weeping?". She said to them, "Because they have taken away my Lord, and I do not know where they have laid him." Saying this she turned round and saw Jesus standing, but she did not know that it was Jesus. Jesus said to her, "Woman, why are you weeping? Whom do you seek?" Supposing him to be the gardener, she said to him, "Sir, if you have carried him away, tell me where you have laid him, and I will take him away." Jesus said to her, "Mary." She turned and said to him in Hebrew, "Rabboni!" (which means Teacher). Jesus said to her, "Do not hold me, for I have not yet ascended to the Father; but go to my brethren and say to them, I am ascending to my Father and your Father, to my God and your God." Mary Magdalene went and said to the disciples, "I have seen the Lord"; and she told them that he had said these things to her. (John 20:1-18)

Meditation on the Resurrection

BY RONDA CHERVIN

✝ I am Mary, the mother of the one who died on the cross. I wanted to die with him. Why didn't he let me die with him?

I do not have to ask long. Missing their Jesus and overwhelmed by guilt, they are coming to me, one by one, weeping on my breast, seeking his forgiveness through mine.

He said it would be terrible during this time. Now I know what he meant. But he also said that there would be victory for us, and that I have yet to fully understand. Is the victory to be here now or only later in heaven? Is what we are witnessing the end of the dream of the Messiah? That after he has come and gone all will appear as if he had never come?

Then I begin to feel his presence; it is growing stronger and stronger. Are the others feeling it also? Some of the women are leaving to go to the grave. I would like to go with them, but my flesh is too weak. I cannot move at all. I am rooted in one place where all the children can find me.

Oh my son! You are coming to them, too. And now I must not only comfort but sustain and encourage them in this joy that is so great that it threatens to be too big for their souls. My broken, open-hearted Mary Magdalene has seen him! She trusts in her vision utterly. Has he not yet ascended to the Father? But he WILL see the rest on the road to Galilee?

Help me up my children, for we must all rejoice! He is risen, as he had promised us! Glory, glory, glory!

The words from the Resurrection scene that have always intrigued me most are the famous "Do not touch me."

What do they imply? First, that before His death Mary Magdalen was privileged to touch Him. He was not a distant figure. Someday He will touch you and me as well, and even now does so in a spiritual way in sacrament and prayer and also by means of human hands.

Yet the words "Do *not* touch me, I have not yet ascended to the Father," also symbolize the way our experience of God goes back and forth between felt closeness and faith in the God behind the veil. "Why? Why? Why?" I used to ask, appalled that the Jesus who had come so near now seemed more a word than a person.

Mary Magdalene's tale and also Mother Mary's have an answer for me. He withdraws so that they may go to minister to Him in the brothers and sisters who will form His mystical body. If we were always caught up in ecstasy, what would give us the impetus to look for love in other creatures. After all, the trip to heaven is not to be a solo voyage, but a pilgrimage in company. And arrival is not only an embrace of a hermit with a lonely God, but rather a joyful banquet of all with their common Saviour.

Discovering the elements of this mystery in love between a man and a woman, we find a tension between the desire to grab and hold onto the other (lust or possessiveness) and the recognition that love is a gift for the lover but also for the community (marriage leads to family).

The young contemplative longs for mystical union with God, but learns that true happiness on earth is meeting Him in the graces of the ordinary as well. So, too, the passionate erotic lover renounces conquest for the tender, steady fire of creative marriage where touch has times and seasons.

Only in eternity will perfect love embrace all longings as all become One.

Meditation on the Resurrection

BY MARY NEILL

"If Christ be not risen," St. Paul says, "our faith is in vain." What can we hope for from the small flame that is our life, our love, if the fire of Christ guttered and darkened forever with his last breath on Calvary? Why should we hope to love again if love died on the cross once and for all?

What did you hope, Mary Magdalene, as you hurried to the garden where they had entombed Christ? Was it that you had enough ointment for the burial rites? That somehow you and your companion would be able to move away the heavy stone? That you might be able to touch Christ's body once more, as you had anointed it in life? That alone, without a crowd around, you could tell him, whether he could hear or not, how much you loved him, how sad you were, how hurt and angry that he had brought you from the death of sin and self-hatred only to leave you alone—no child, no husband, no lover?

Alone again. Your taut heart urges you to the tomb. Just to touch him once more and wrap him away in death; seeing him might make the pain ease some, or burst out in a great cleansing gush. Your mind swirls: just to touch him once more; him who had not rejected your touch, who had healed you with his touch. Just once more.

And then, you see the empty tomb, and hope drains away. Sobbing then, you see him dimly, first as gardener, then as "Rabboni," when he calls your name. You *hear* him before you can see him. He is not inaccessible, you can hear his command. But he is changed; you cannot touch him, cannot cling to him. As suddenly gone as there, he fades from your sight, telling you to *go* to the brethren; that your renewed energy is for them—not for yourself or even him.

To see him again, however changed, to know that he lives to guide your way, to feel his love for you enflame your heart—all of this is more than you had hoped for, and also less. To have touched a dead Christ would have meant an end, a closure perhaps easier than this door that remains ajar, beckoning. "I open and no man closes," he said. And you must leave the tomb of closure.

Strange, compelling teacher who opens doors when one thinks them closed, he who is word made flesh, giving his flesh for food. Appearing after death first to you, a woman whose trade was your flesh. He lives on enfleshed in the Church you must serve. First preacher of the resurrections, you must anoint and guard this Church's flesh as you would his own; you must not cling to the flesh you have known, but to that which needs your faith, your hope, your love—your dogged courage and flaming passion now.

What release you must have felt when, in a flash, what he really meant, what he was all about became clear. His large heart had freed your small heart trapped in small cornered rooms, parcelled and sold in bits. Your heart grew large enough for his free spirit as it roved and loved in Galilee. Now returned from death, his command is that you must make your heart larger now, large as the world—larger than the man you knew as him. Large as God. There is no limit now to whom and how and when you shall love, in whose face and eyes you shall see Christ's flesh needing you, loving you back.

When you told the apostles the good news and felt their dismissal of you as over-wrought from sorrow, I imagine you returning to the quiet of that garden to think about Jesus. It no longer matters so much if you see his face again; you feel his love flaming in your heart. Is it your heart anymore? You wonder: Is it not rather his that beats in your heart?

Tradition says that you wandered far from Israel and became a contemplative seeing his face in every gardener, every rose, every thorn. Some must have thought you "strange," touching everything so gently, so tenderly, as if you saw it fresh from God's hands—or as the flesh of God himself. I would like to have touched you, or seen your eyes as they looked at things. Eyes that had seen debauchery, degradation, and death—and God's face turned toward you in love.

Mary Magdalene, I pray to you to help me love the Church, for Jesus called you to love and serve the Church. If I am to love the Lord, I must love his bride, and I with difficulty see His face in hers. Her sins seem to me not sins of the flesh, but of fear against the flesh; confinement of life, spirit, spontaneity.

Abundant life, renewed life that is Jesus risen, enlarge my heart, teach me to touch tenderly all flesh, all life; teach me not to cling to old forms, or loved ones who must go their own way. Teach me to wait in the garden of my soul for Christ's calling my name—help me live the largeness of the Resurrection in the size of what I hope for; keep me from settling for too little.

The Mystery of the Ascension
Coming Home

To them he presented himself alive after his passion by many
proofs, appearing to them during forty days, and speaking of
the kingdom of God. And while staying with them he charged
them not to depart from Jerusalem, but to wait for the promise
of the Father which, he said, "you heard from me, for John
baptized with water, but before many days you shall be baptized with the Holy Spirit."

So when they had come together, they asked him, "Lord,
will you at this time restore the kingdom to Israel?" He said to
them, "It is not for you to know times or seasons which the Father has fixed by his own authority. But you shall receive
power when the Holy Spirit has come upon you; and you shall
be my witnesses in Jerusalem and in all Judea and Samaria and
to the end of the earth." And when he had said this, as they
were looking on, he was lifted up, and a cloud took him out of
their sight. And while they were gazing into heaven as he went,
behold, two men stood by them in white robes, and said, "Men
of Galilee, why do you stand looking into heaven? This Jesus,
who was taken up from you into heaven, will come in the same
way as you saw him go into heaven."

Then they returned to Jerusalem from the mount called
Olivet, which is near Jerusalem, a sabbath day's journey away;
and when they had entered, they went up to the upper room
where they were staying . . . All these with one accord devoted
themselves to prayer. (Acts 1:3–14)

Meditation on the Ascension

BY RONDA CHERVIN

✝ We are all assembled on the mountain for the last farewell. Sadness mingles with awe, for who has seen such a leave-taking since Elijah's?! It is a moment of triumphant glory for me, although I am saddened that I will not see his transfigured, luminous face until my end has come.

After he rose from the grave, mad confusion as well as joyous victory overcame the disciples. First, they were jumpy with panic, not knowing what they were to do. The city was teeming with wild rumors. Groups gathered in swarms around anyone who knew him so as to discover whether the incredible news of his rising was true. Moreover, people wanted to know if they could meet him. To this we could not answer, because Jesus would appear unexpectedly, coming and going even through closed doors.

When he was amongst us, he instructed his disciples about what was to come and how to go about teaching his story. I loved to listen to him as he traced the history and meaning of his coming through the holy books. He spoke to me when the others slept, for I was always awake when he wanted me. He told me many secrets of the kingdom and of the times when they would be revealed to man, in order that I might be prepared. I was to channel the needs and hopes of man to God and God to man through the hidden pathways of inner prayer. I was to be the pure light of Jesus in the world so that those who would come to me would leave me strengthened.

Now he is embracing each of us, with extra warmth for the ones who need it the most, especially Peter, who will be the rock of his kingdom.

They told me later it was like the time of his transfiguration on Mount Tabor, when he stood, glorious, white as snow, conversing with Moses and Elijah. His already translucent body shone brighter and brighter until he then streaked up in a blinding flash of light into the heavens. We stared upwards, each one of us sharing the same thought: When would we be following and joining him? And then an angel came and told us to return to the city.

My soul is dazed and my spirit waits in delighted anticipation for the time when I and my dear children will receive the Holy Spirit as he promised. I, knowing this gift, am eager to see my children grow in grace and truth.

Come let us sing as we walk towards the holy city. The Lord has risen and we are rising towards him, forever and ever.

The eternal home is pure gift. We cannot merit it, although we may reject it. C.S. Lewis conjectured that heaven and hell are not two different places with different aims. There is one eternity, God, and for some, his absolute love is hell; for others, heaven.

But what if we hate to regard our happiness as gift and want it instead to be our own achievement? Then we refuse the mystery of the Ascension and seek a God within oneself, controllable by ourselves. We make our own experiences into deities for worship. We buy the pseudo-eternity of sensual, emotional, and spiritual thrills, as something we can have and manipulate rather than receive from a being higher than ourselves.

Another type of refusal of the eternal home is what Sören Kierkegaard in *The Sickness unto Death* called the despair of finitude. Afraid that the eternal homeland may be hoax, we cling fiercely to the reality of the here and now. We imagine that certain earthly goods can satisfy forever, and, when these fail to do so, we seek new kinds of satisfaction. When all fails, we curse life, but still refuse to raise our eyes toward the heavens.

So what can the account of the Ascension mean to those who no longer believe in an eternal afterlife, to those whose life is but a round trip from nothingness to nothingness? What does eternity mean anyhow? *Eternity*—that word has always thrilled me, even as an atheist when I yet had no knowledge of a heavenly destiny.

I regard eternity not as a dissolution of time, but rather as the temporal rolled up into a perfect point of ecstasy in which all things become unified in the heart of God. How do I know what it is like? I have glimpsed it in my own experience of moments when time seems to stop and all the beauty and goodness and love and truth of the world are gathered up and concentrated into one brilliant vision and explosion of feeling. It can happen anywhere, anytime. Sometimes it has happened at the ocean or on a mountaintop, but just as easily at the sight of a familiar object on a busy day. The ordinary things become suffused with the presence of the absolute. "Earth's crammed with heaven, and every common bush afire with God," wrote Elizabeth Barret Browning.

My vision of eternity was very philosophical in quality until C.S. Lewis' writings "baptized my imagination" with visions of the new heaven and the new earth full of all the beautiful things that I love on earth tinctured with the light of God's glory and destiny given to them.

Once I looked up *eternity* in the Catholic Encyclopedia. I was amazed by the number of descriptions it offered. On so important an issue, theologians have long differed in explanations. Some stress the beatific vision, a pure absorption in the glory of God, and others, the transformation of the natural world to full obedience to the Creator who can then reign as true Lord. St. Thomas Aquinas upholds both views, for within their union with God, all good things on earth will be known and fully enjoyed.

Eternity is the beatific vision, the most abundant life possible to creatures, the return to the mother, as well as to the father. From God in his maternity as well as paternity, all things have proceeded and will return.

Meditation on the Ascension

BY MARY NEILL

"Christ, ascending on high, led captivity captive." In early preaching of the gospel, the death, Resurrection, and Ascension of Jesus were all one mystery—that of the glorification of Christ. "Now is the hour come to glorify me, Father," Christ prayed. What does this "glory" mean? I wonder. "My soul gives glory to God," Mary sang. How can we come to understand this consciousness of glory the scriptures speak of that the Ascension centrally celebrates?

If Christ prayed for glorification, if he captured glory, it was that we too might come to this gift. How can I pray for this conformity to the mind of Christ, unless I try to imagine it, to experience it however dimly in the events of my own life? For me, homecomings have been "glory" moments. Seeing the first rays of sunlight break over the horizon when I was watching and waiting, and hearing the swelling of voices in music — these bring glory too.

Is this what your Ascension was, Jesus, homecoming for you; the star rise which knew no setting, yesterday, today, or forever? Was it all the voices out from the past saying, "You are ours; your love has made our suffering and death meaningful because you died for all, you lived best of all and gave form to our living and dying."

Jesus, in ascending you make the past and the future your home. "I go to prepare you a home," you tell your disciples. You go to make of all the wide cosmos a home. No more need men and women feel lost in this world; they have a home in you, who have ascended to the heights and plumbed the depths.

"Only he who has descended may ascend," the scriptures say. Is that our task posed by this mystery — to risk the heights of joy and glory as well as the depths of pain and loss? Because you descended deep into your earthbound humanity, into your own time and land, you could reach above the earth and beyond time. You have dared to move through the circle of all the elements — earth, air, fire, and water. Pinned to the earth on the cross, flooded with sorrow, burned in the crucible of suffering, now you become master of the air, the wind, the stars — moving through the skies. Jesus *Ichthyths*, sacred fish and fisher of men, you swim in all the elements and you call us to master the earth, air, fire, and water that season our souls with their entombment, flight, burning, and inundations.

What did you see, Jesus, as you looked up to the heavens? What glory drew you home? Was it the eyes of Abraham brimming for the Isaac you had become? Moses' smile at your out-lawing his law by the law of love; Joseph the dreamer seeing all dreams filled in you. The "Abba, Father" that was pain now becomes "Abba, Father" that is glory. "Jesus is music in the ear, honey on the tongue and a shout of gladness in the heart," St. Bernard says. Ascension is that shout of gladness in all the hearts for whom you are the Alpha and the Omega, all who were made captives in Adam's fall.

An ancient homily for Holy Saturday imagines you touching Adam:

> The earth has trembled and fallen still, for the Lord sleeps in his fleshly nature; in the netherworld he is arousing those who have slept for ages. God is dead in the flesh, and has shaken sheol to its foundations. He goes to seek our first parent like a lost sheep. He wills to visit those who sit in the dark shadows of death and to release Adam and his wife from their grievous captivity. The Lord takes Adam's hand and says to him, "Wake, sleeper, and rise from the dead, and Christ shall enlighten you. I am your God. For your sake I became one of your sons: to you now and to all your posterity I say, Go forth! You who are in darkness, look upon the light! You who sleep, rise up! I bid you: Awake, sleeper! I did not create you to lie bound in hell. Arise from the dead, for I am life to those who have died. Rise up, work of my hands, my likeness, made in my image. Rise, let us go hence. . . . Arise, let us go hence. I have a heavenly throne prepared for you, and the cherubim shall bow down before you.

"Rise up", you say to Adam's children again and again. As you fade from sight of the trembling disciples, afraid, unsure, not knowing the glory they have within, you say, "Rise up." "Go give the waters of baptism, the fire of love, the earth rock of fidelity, the fresh air of hope, gladness, and glory. Tell the good news that glory has been revealed in weakness, death, and darkness; that earth cannot entomb, fire destroy, water drown, nor air evaporate the spirit of man evolved to the white heat of divinity in my heart."

I feel the sorrow and the anguish of the disciples when they realize that they will see you fleshly never more as your presence grows thin as air, fading, up, up, up — a star to see, but not to touch. One does not grab glory; one waits to bathe in it, as in the first rays of sun. The psalmist sings, "Mount high above the heavens, God, until your glory overshadows the earth"(Ps. 56).

And I pray to you Lord Jesus, seated in glory at the right hand of the Father, ready to give us the power to plumb the depths and the heights,

- help me to move freely in the movement from depth to height, from height to depth.
- help me to know that your power will sustain me through the vertigo of life's cycles.
- let me not be afraid to be transformed into air, into breath, wind, and movement.
- release me from the captivities in my depths; bring me captive to your home in glory; help me not fear your glory nor mine.

The Descent of the Holy Spirit
Loving Unconditionally

When the day of Pentecost had come, they were all together in one place. And suddenly a sound came from heaven like the rush of a mighty wind, and it filled all the house where they were sitting. And there appeared to them tongues as of fire, distributed and resting on each one of them. And they were all filled with the Holy Spirit and began to speak in other tongues, as the Spirit gave them utterance.

Now there were dwelling in Jerusalem Jews, devout men from every nation under heaven. And at this sound the multitude came together, and they were bewildered, because each one heard them speaking in his own language. And they were amazed and wondered, saying, "Are not all these who are speaking Galileans? And how is it that we hear, each of us in his own native language? Parthians and Medes and Elamites and residents of Mesopotamia, Judea and Cappodocia, Pontus and Asia, Phrygia and Pamphylia, Egypt and the parts of Libya belonging to Cyrene, and visitors from Rome, both Jews and proselytes, Cretans and Arabians, we hear them telling in our own tongues the mighty works of God." And all were amazed and perplexed.... And he [Peter] testified with many other words and exhorted them, saying, "Save yourselves from this crooked generation." So those who received his word were baptized, and there were added that day about three thousand souls.   (Acts 2:1-12, 40-41)

Meditation on the Descent of the Holy Spirit

BY RONDA CHERVIN

✝ We are in the upper room again, all together: the disciples of Jesus, Mary Magdalen and the other women Jesus loved, and myself. The pressure is growing upon us to move outside, to take the daring plunge and proclaim good news openly to all in the streets. I have been restraining them, gently but firmly reminding them that Jesus told them to wait for the Holy Spirit. But they can hardly bear to wait any longer.

And now we are gathered together, praying. Suddenly, a wind sweeps around the room and something like flames of fire come pouring down upon us! We begin to weep and groan, exploding in new tongues! The room can no longer contain us and we fling ourselves out of the room, fearlessly, joyously proclaiming the message of glory, glory, glory! Thousands from the wondering crowd who gathered to listen to us are added to Jesus's followers that day. The power of the kingdom is upon us now. I embrace each son and daughter and bless them all. I am the mother of the Church.

What is the fire-rain of new life in the Holy Spirit that comes after tears of emptiness? When I first became Catholic, the terms used to name the gifts of the Holy Spirit were largely unknown. I had never heard of tongues, interpretation, prophecy, or healing, much less imagined the possibility of their manifesting themselves in modern times. Elaborate analogical explanations were used to make these biblical terms relevant to modern ears.

Then the revival of Pentecostal movements in Protestant and Catholic circles alike transformed the situation, making these "terms" burning realities for me and many other Christians.

But whatever our experience of the gifts of the Holy Spirit, St. Paul, the greatest charismatic Christian of them all, insisted that the most important gift of the Holy Spirit is love. "Love," Paul wrote, "is patient; love is kind. Love is not jealous, it does not put on airs, it is not snobbish. Love is never rude, it is not self-seeking, it is not prone to anger; neither does it brood over injuries. Love does not rejoice in what is wrong but rejoices with the truth. There is no limit to love's forebearance, to its trust, its hope, its power to endure." (1 Corinthians 13:4-7)

Love is the chief gift of the Holy Spirit. "Love never fails. Prophecies will cease, tongues will be silent, knowledge will pass away. Our knowledge is imperfect and our prophesying is imperfect." (1 Corinthians 13:8-10) And blessed with an abundance of such a gift as the Holy Spirit, the greatest fruit of the work of the Holy Spirit upon us will also be love.

How do the gifts of the Holy Spirit mesh with the fruits (which include besides love, "joy, peace, patient endurance, kindness, generosity, faith, mildness, and chastity.") (Galatians 5:22) How can searing fire bring forth soothing spring rains? The secret is cyclic. The yearning for the Spirit, for God, fills us and then overflows in tender concern for others.

This process of spiritual alchemy may be refused for quite different reasons: We may refuse from the spirit of compromise which calls for only a small flame so as not to disturb the tranquility of serving mammon; or we may refuse by the roaring fire of fanaticism which is devoid of any cooling, calming waters for oneself or for others. In fanaticism, we bring to the lives of others a fire that, rather than enkindling or inspiring enthusiam for God, ravages them in our merciless, single-minded determination to root out all evil. We become St. Paul before the Damascus encounter. Our fire blinds us and destroys others. Finally, we can cling to so-called private visions that we have received from the Holy Spirit. Rather than revealing them to the world when called upon to do so, or growing spiritually as a result of them to better love and serve others, we choose to hoard them miserly to ourselves for personal comfort and satisfaction.

Meditation on the Holy Spirit

BY MARY NEILL

Come, Holy Spirit. I have often prayed those words and yet you elude me as person. I have felt the person of the Father and the person that is Jesus; why is it so hard to feel your person? You are the love that leaps between Father and Son, the fire that falls at Pentecost, unfreezing cowardly hearts, unlocking frightened tongues. You are a dove and gentle, a fire and warm, a wind and refreshing, a breath that exhilarates; you take all forms and have no form; you have one thousand faces and no face.

How can I love your mystery? How can I open to your love that has no face? I dreamed once of walking along the beach with my mother, and her face was covered by a mask. Pondering the dream, it came to me that in a sense my fleshly mother was the masked carrier, the vessel, the "front" for all the mothering love of God that brought forth the universe. This is the spirit of nurture at play in the world, tender and caring, quick to protect as my own mother has been to me in our essential bondedness.

You, Holy Spirit, bonded in fire those disciples flooded with fear. Christ bonded them in truth, but truth was not enough. How quickly our insights and truths falter before the unraveling struggles of our existence. How could the disciples face the world, face one another, face themselves even with the truth of Christ's memory if they were not branded and bonded, melded with tongues of fire, Holy Spirit, a fire no waters of distance and sorrow can quench.

I imagine myself locked in that upper room, imploded with sadness and impotence. I feel, at first slowly and gently, then strongly and fiercely, the wind of love unlocking my tongue and heart. I look to see in Mary's eyes; then, in Peter, James, and John lightening love leaps back so that we are not locked each in our solitary dream and betrayal, but we have now the same dream, a common language. Isolates have become a WE; each face and heart is

Christ's face, is my face. I lose my mask, my imaginary face, and become part of that homeland of hearts that is the Church, born now not only from Christ's side, but from our hearts and tongues.

"The spirit whom I will send will teach you all things." This Spirit teaches us the one thing necessary — unconditional love. The sin against the Spirit will be to disbelieve in His unconditional love. I can preach Christ not because I have understood Him perfectly or followed Him without sin, but because I cannot deny the effects of this love poured forth in me, a sea ever pounding on the shore of my rocky, land-bound self distrust. The Father called my name, creating me in my mother's womb; Jesus calls my name in the garden of my pain and His; the Spirit calls my name in every locked room.

Each name is different, as He who calls is a different person; Father calls me child; Christ calls me bride; Spirit calls me woman. If I do not know your face, Holy Spirit, it's because perhaps I have not known my face as woman. Until I have that face, will your person elude me?

So, Holy Spirit, I pray,

- Show me your face in all the faces that I meet; your love carving out the mystery of the Father and the Son in every life.
- Help me not to be afraid to be woman, fully mortal, fully alive, fully loved and loving.
- Show me gently all the locked rooms of fear that need opening to your love.
- Help me know the Church as a homeland of hearts; help me make it such by my fidelity and love.

The Mystery of Assumption
Bringing the Mother Home

Meditation on the Assumption

BY RONDA CHERVIN

✝ I am Mary. Years have passed since I witnessed the coming of the Holy Spirit in the upper chamber. My sons and daughters have scattered in all directions stretching out to the glorious dance of grace. Here I remain in the heart of the holy city, contemplating the kingdom of heaven and earth.

Somedays I feel so close to my Son now in heaven that my feet seem to leave the earth. Other days I am so close to the daily struggles of his mission that I seem to be rooted and bound in earth.

Oh, the angel has come again! As he came to me at the beginning of my Son's story on earth. "Hail, full of grace, blessed art thou!" In a few months, he proclaims, the Holy Spirit will overshadow me and I shall see my Son again in glory. In full glory this time! The heavens will open and I will be lifted up, body and soul, like my Son, to him.

But until then, I must bid the earth farewell. As I wait, my gaze searches the earth for all that is worthy of heaven. I will bring to God the lilies of the field, the birds of the air, the hearts of the lov-

94

ing, the sorrows of the poor, the innocence of children. And when the time has come for my departure, the angels will come to take me up from my poor pallet. I will have embraced my children for the last time and fallen asleep, to awake under the shelter of wings being drawn up by dancing angels to my eternal home where my Son reigns in glory. Glory to God in the highest: God, the Father, Son, and Holy Spirit! Alleluia!

I have always envisioned the Assumption as the climax of a dance. Mary, suspended between earth and heaven, is the ballerina being lifted up, her back arched over the uplifted arms of her partner.

In the perfect moments of dance performances, the body and spirit become one as both leap in harmony with the soaring crescendoes of passionate melodies. Audiences count the number of seconds a dancer can remain elevated in the air before descending. Grace of form evokes grace of spirit. At the apex of all grace, why should not the body and spirit finally soar into eternity? "The pure souls shall mount on native wings, disdaining little sport, and cut a path into the heaven of glory, leaving a track of light for men to wonder at," wrote William Blake.

The doctrine of the resurrection of the body, proclaimed every Sunday in countless recitations of the Creed, is still strange to people so repulsed at the thought, and even more the sight, of corpses. It is much easier to imagine souls flying to heaven than bodies mysteriously transfigured leaping up to join their soul-mates on the last day!

The scriptures shine light on the mystery. Jesus after his Resurrection had a body that was hard to recognize as the one which he had before he died, yet this resurrected body was firm enough to be probed, and could eat and drink. "The mystery of the Assumption teaches us that in Mary, the transfiguration of the cosmos, the principle of which lies in the Resurrection of Christ, has already begun to produce its effect. The Assumption is the dawn of the new creation whose first rays filter through into the darkness of the world," wrote Jean Danielou.

Those who reject life after death usually cling with desperate fingers to what can be seen and touched. They cannot release themselves to the stream that takes them to destinations unknown. Those who reject the body insult the Creator who insisted that what He lovingly created was good. Why does man exist as matter in a material world at all if only his spirit counts to God? The Assumption of Our Lady is shrouded in mystery. An aprocryphal fourth century book of that name described it in detail. The doctrine appears to have sprung from common belief among early Christians. Theologians derive it from the implications of the immaculate conception: If Mary is full of grace, as Luke describes the angel Gabriel proclaiming, then she is free of original sin, and thus not subject to the punishment of having her body corrupt on earth before being raised on the last day. She is said to have fallen into a death-like sleep called the Dormition by the Fathers of the Church, and then disappeared, body and soul, into heaven.

For the development of Christian spirituality, the doctrine of the Assumption has profound consequences. All creation was groaning for redemption and Mary's ascent prefigures the time when all that is good of the earth will be drawn up into heaven. At that time man's body, rather than being discarded for the next waltz, will become the most graceful instrument conceivable to perform the dance of union with God for all eternity.

Meditation on the Assumption

BY MARY NEILL

If the Annunciation is plainsong, virginal solitude pregnant with hidden life, the Assumption is polyphonic chorus, a thousand voices singing, "Rejoice you angels and bless the Lord; Mary has been raised to heaven." Strange mystery of opposites again: old woman's death on earth, now renewed flesh elevated with angels. Mary's body is rarely painted by the masters as old; is this agist sexism or the eternal renewal and youth embodied in the feminine principle?

I understand, Mary, why the Church has always believed that your body which created Christ's body should be brought with His to heaven, but I have never known what this mystery challenges me to do, or to be, for the mystery is not an ornament, but an image of being. So, Mary, help me understand about sleeping in death, for this feast was first called the Dormition, the sleeping of Mary. Help me understand the heavenly love that longs for bodies to meet; I understand why earthly sons long for their mother's arms. And teach me about angels—for it is angels who bring you tidings of Christ's birth, angels who rejoice when your body is brought to the Lord. All these images are so far from my modern mind; what is the wisdom my ancestors learned from them?

Is it that heaven wants warm bodies as much as we earth-bound creatures want heaven? Is there an opposite pulling us there? Is it that heaven is not home without a mother, and a mother is no mother without her body—legs and arms and breast and lap? That Jesus got His mother back in every way because He separated freely from her—"Who is my mother?" He said. You had desired to be with Him and had been rebuffed; now your desire is His.

Wordsworth called you "our tainted nature's solitary boast"; the Church declares you immaculately conceived, ever pure in mind and heart and body. How can I reach you, covered with glorious titles, assumed further and further away from my world. You seem close and mine when I think of you at the crib or at the cross; these are human categories. But I cannot reach you pure and heavenly. Why would you want to reach to me, impure and earth-bound?

So, humanly, I picture you dying. Wrinkled and gray-headed, forgetful in your old age, repeating stories already told, worrying about John and Peter and James and all the band bonded in fire at Pentecost, you fade little by little, less in this world, more in the world to come or the world that was. Children love to sit by your side and feel your steady flame of love, your gentleness and warmth. You laugh a lot, or smile to hear their whispered secrets and cares that become lighter in your presence.

They want to hear about Jesus and you tell them simple little things, perhaps disappointing them with no hyperbole. He was, you say, a fine man, God's son and yours, content to walk the earth and laugh and cry and care and talk and die, true to His Father in heaven and to you. But not easy to understand. "I understand Him better now," you say, "but I still have much to ponder." You fall silent, and in a while they see you silent, eyes closed, and wonder if you are asleep or dead. Old people often look dead when they sleep. And one day they find you and they cannot wake you from your sleep. "She's with Him at last," they say; "She'll look after us still better there than here," and they comfort one another in their loss.

The sleep of Mary that is a doorway to life; the disciples must nurture one another with you gone. How lovingly they touch your body in death, grateful for the power that flows from you still—a power that cannot keep you locked in earth: your being, your story, your body must, for them and for us, become a star whose light pulsates beyond death.

O Mary, help me understand about bodies—how to venerate them, love them, honor them; help me know a purity that is not sterility but life, abundant and radiant beyond decay.

O Mary, let me know that God's power flows throughout the universe, drawing all things to completion in Him. Let me not deny that power. O Mary, help me give my burden of perfectionism to you; if you are "tainted nature's solitary boast," then I don't have to be.

The Mystery of the Crowning
of Mary Queen of Heaven
Hoping Brought Full Circle

And a great portent appeared in heaven, a woman clothed with the sun, with the moon under her feet, and on her head a crown of twelve stars; she was with child and she cried out in her pangs of birth, in anguish for delivery. And another portent appeared in heaven; behold a great red dragon, with seven heads and ten horns, and seven diadems upon his heads. His tail swept down a third of the stars of heaven, and cast them to the earth. And the dragon stood before the woman who was about to bear a child, and that he might devour her child when she brought it forth; she brought forth a male child, one who is to rule all the nations with a rod of iron, but her child was caught up to God and to his throne, and the woman fled into the wilderness, where she has a place prepared by God, in which to be nourished for one thousand two hundred and sixty days.   (Rev. 12:1-6)

Meditation on the Mystery of the Crowning

BY RONDA CHERVIN

Praise you, Virgin Mary, who let the strong be weak;
Praise you, Mother Mary, who made the weak strong.
Praise you, Virgin Mary, who crushed the serpent's head;
Praise you, Mother Mary, refuge of sinners.
Praise you, Virgin Mary, Bride of the Spirit;
Praise you, Mother Mary, Mother of the Living and the Dead.
Praise you, Virgin Mary, lamp of Israel;
Praise you, Mother Mary, star of the Kingdom.

Oh Mary, teach your daughters to believe in glory,
Yours and ours!
Take away our self-denigrating and despairing disbelief.
Help us to place our sorrows in your lap.
For the joys you offer us are fragrant flowers in your hair,
And the glories you bestow on us, gems in your crown!
Oh, Mary, it is with litanies that we your children crown you,
    overwhelmed with the extravagance of your gifts.
We murmur over and over Queen, Mother, Rose, Tower of
    Ivory,
Seat of Wisdom, as in the Litany I now sing anew:

Litany of the Blessed Virgin
Lord, have mercy on us. Christ, have mercy on us.
Christ, hear us. Christ, graciously hear us.
God, the Father of Heaven, have mercy on us.
God, the Son, Redeemer of the world, have mercy on us.
God, the Holy Spirit, have mercy on us.
Holy Trinity, one God, have mercy on us.
Holy Mary, pray for us. (*Repeated after each invocation*)
Holy Mother of God,
Holy Virgin of virgins,

Mother of Christ,
Mother of divine grace,
Mother most pure,
Mother most chaste,
Mother inviolate,
Mother undefiled,
Mother most amiable,
Mother most admirable,
Mother of good Counsel,
Mother of our Creator,
Mother of our Savior,
Virgin most prudent,
Virgin most venerable,
Virgin most renowned,
Virgin most powerful,
Virgin most merciful,
Virgin most faithful,
Mirror of justice,
Seat of wisdom,
Cause of our joy,
Spriritual vessel,
Vessel of honor,
Singular vessel of devotion,
Mystical rose,
Tower of David,
Tower of ivory,
House of gold,
Ark of the covenant,
Gate of heaven,
Morning star,
Health of the sick,
Refuge of sinners,
Comforter of the afflicted,
Help of Christians,
Queen of Angels,
Queen of Patriarchs,

Queen of Prophets,
Queen of Apostles,
Queen of Martyrs,
Queen of Confessors,
Queen of Virgins,
Queen of all Saints,
Queen, conceived without original sin,
Queen, assumed into Heaven,
Queen of the most holy Rosary,
Queen of Peace.
Lamb of God, who take away the sins of the world,
Spare us, O Lord. Lamb of God, who take away the sins
of the world, graciously hear us, O Lord. Lamb of God . . .
have mercy on us.

My wonder at your mystery, Mary, began before my conversion.

The first statue I saw of the Virgin Mary was on the campus of Fordham University in New York. I was startled that a college would have a statue, not of Einstein or Newton or Plato, but, instead, of a robed figure, half-child, half-woman, doing nothing except extending her palms upward in a gesture of receptivity.

As I got to know Catholic men, I was amazed at the attachment they had for the mysterious Mary. My godfather could not pass a picture of Mary without tears filling his eyes. Tough Catholic boys carried rosaries in the frayed pockets of their jeans next to their knives. Why? Reflecting on the words of the rosary prayer, ". . . blessed is the fruit of your womb. . . . holy Mary, mother of God . . . pray for us sinners now and at the hour of our death . . .," I came to understand that man, who has no womb, was yet born from a womb and ever seeks the protective warmth of the feminine. He turns to the women in his life and to his heavenly mother to heal the wounds the world has inflicted on him. The feminine teaches him to put love before the competitiveness he falls into in pursuing his role as provider. The figure of the heavenly mother on the altar draws him out of weariness into the hope of the promises of the kingdom where there will be for all, women and men, no more toil and tears, only joy!

Paintings of Mary have played a crucial role in my life. I love the famous Botticelli Annunciation, where the angel starts the dance and Mary bends backwards in ecstasy. I love the flaming Grunewald Madonna, with her flowing blondish-red hair, in a brilliant red velvet gown, her eyes gazing down in utterly peaceful joy at the gift of God held in her long slender hands. Most of all, I love the unfinished sepia-colored Da Vinci Nativity. I, an untamed sensual girl, first discovered the beauty of purity upon gazing at the simple, girlish outline of this virgin Madonna in a museum in Florence, Italy, and shed the tears that began the cleansing of my heart.

At Fordham University, Father Donceel, the well-known Jesuit theologian-philosopher, used to begin the class with the Our Father followed by the phrase, "Seat of Wisdom, pray for us." I was perplexed. What was the seat of wisdom? Oh, that woman, Mary. How could a village girl with no graduate degrees be the seat of wisdom?!

Then I learned about contemplation. I had never heard of the word before. I was told that the lyrical, poetic side of me, with its luminous images hidden deep in my heart, this soft blissful inner-me, counted as much, if not more, than the me who churned out term paper after term paper of well-organized concepts. Deep within me was the source of wisdom. Joy, Joy, Joy!

Your title Our Lady, Star of the Sea also attracted me. I have rarely been at sea, but the name Our Lady, Star of the Sea on churches in beach towns has always moved me: the contrast between the raging waves and the still, silent woman — the image of strong men in small boats rowing towards the harbor, towards the waiting woman, glowing in the darkness, hands outstretched in welcome. The feminine is the refuge.

The child flees from the danger of the streets to home which means Mama. Before descending into the fiery waves of nightmare images, Mother must tuck her babies snug into their beds. They must know that anytime in the night they can flee to the parental bed. Even as adults, in fright they call for Mama.

This universal need for refuge and comfort, is it to be scorned as weak, whining self-pity? I think not. Self-pity is nurtured in lonely brooding. The one who acknowledges her vulnerability and fear and feels reassured in the fact that there are mothers to tend her wounds, is far less prone to whining.

I resented it when the often sentimental statues of Mary were pitched out of the churches, to be replaced by jagged, triangular glass shapes, coldly beautiful, but chilling for the child in man. Then Mother Mary came back to me personally in the form of the women of the prayer groups, encircling the heaving, battered forms of each other with embraces of compassion. I became mother over and over again kissing the cheeks of women whose tears had smeared away their cosmetic masks and of men whose stoicism cracked at the miraculous touch of sisters and brothers who were unafraid to be tender. Soothed, they were ready to join us in the circle to rescue the next supplicant.

Meditation on the Crowning of Mary as Queen of Heaven

BY MARY NEILL

Once, I felt I was queen for an hour when 6000 people stood and cheered when I got an award. I carried a sceptre and led a procession and people smiled when they saw me. It was a fine moment — everyone should have such a moment when she is queen and others smile to see her face and her robe of power falls easy on her shoulders and theirs.

And once, too, I saw the Queen of England, Elizabeth II, and she looked completely queenly — white satin, purple velvet, ermine and diamonds, gold sceptre. I cried when we sang "God Save Our Queen" because she was there safe and smiling and she liked it. She accepted being loved, with the crowds on corners waiting to catch her eye and see her hand wave ever so slightly, as befits a queen. I thought at the time: Oh, I wish we had a queen. And so we do in you, Mary.

"To the queen of hearts is the ace of sorrows," goes the ballad. And so I wonder what I would have seen in your face and form as you were crowned Queen of Heaven and Earth. Would there be some sorrow lingering in your eyes still, souvenirs of old wars? A compassion and a depth that would draw the beholder? Are you different as queen than you were as girl, as bride, as woman of sorrows? I would like to paint you if I could, or bring you flowers on a rainy day. I would stand a long time on a corner to see you smile and wave your hand.

Why is feminine power so beautiful? Liquid grace and ease and warmth, freedom and flow, earth, air, and fire reflected on the water that is woman. The water mirrors them all — light and movement, buoyancy, containment, floating, floating — all the sea's movement and power evoke the queenly hand.

No wonder we hasten to call you Star of the Sea, fire reflecting on water. I read that our ancestor's pre-ancestors came from the sea, that the fluid in our veins has the same salts as those in the seas. When I look at the sea and throw to her my confusion and fear, she takes them as my mother and hides them in her faithful ebb and tide which soothes me with its receding roar. The sea is queen, and I am strengthened by bathing in the reflection of her waters.

Are you, as Queen of Heaven, the sea become person; are you the waters from above become separate for the waters below? I am comforted that you are my queen and mother; like the sea, you will not fail. I, too, will not fail, but endure all the tides and seasons, all the elements of earth, air, fire, and water, for as you were made of heaven and for heaven and brought full circle crowned with sorrow and with glory, so I am made not only of sea salts, but made of heaven, for heaven.

"Our life, our sweetness and our hope," we sing in the Salve moaning over the "O mild, O devout, O sweet Virgin Mary." Oh, we who are in the valley of tears are pulled from its darkness by the thought of you who passed through the dark colors as passage and not as grave. First Christian, first lady at the cross, first to be crowned, pray for all of us seconds, thirds, and fourths, and millionths who are too much at home in the dark valley and not enough in the high heaven.

- Help me to know to whom I pledge my loyalties, whom I serve, whose colors I wear.
- Let me bow down before the glory of the feminine, willing to wear its liquid graces.

✝ Part Two

BRINGING THE MOTHER WITH YOU

"Who is my mother?"

Bringing the Mother with You

BY MARY NEILL

"Who is my mother?" Jesus asks, the strange question that probes the listener. The Church, that mothering institution through the centuries, has lovingly and urgently answered his question.

Mary is the first Christian; she who first believed that God was with us — with her in a profoundly new way — a light whose darkness would not be extinguished; a power of life and healing, the hallmark of God himself; she is God's mother, we even dare to say.

He who fathered forth all things in Jesus and through Jesus, has given Himself a mother in Mary, and gives her to us. Mother of God. What kind of God is it who would have a mother? Strange mystery. "Mater dei et Mater gratiae, Mater veniae, Mater plena sanctae laetitiae." "Mother of God, of grace, of small things, mother full of holy happiness," the medieval chant sings of her.

Amazing. If I were God's mother, what would that mean? Would I know it? How did she know it? How am I to mother forth God to the world? We are told that Mary is assumed into heaven, that she is immaculately conceived. What does that mean for me? If she does first what I am to do, how will I follow to those sacred gardens? I don't exactly know. How can I further ponder why

Christians have said these things about Mary? How may I honor more their inner meaning? How can I help so many in the modern church who have lost Mary, and the strength given by the ancient devotions? Is she now like the one in the story of the Good Samaritan who has been beaten and robbed of her worth, left to die by the wayside, passed, ignored by priest and Levite. Am I called — is the Church called — to save her from this injury? Will the Tibetan, the Hindu, the Protestant who never crowned her with blossoms in May see her worth before we do, busy as we are on the way to Jericho?

"And the walls came tumbling down."

Bringing the Mother with You

BY RONDA CHERVIN

Dear Mother Mary, I hear you chant this lullaby to me:

Come to me, daughter of Eve,
Seek shelter under my wings.
Let my mothering envelop you.
Become yourself mother to others, then;
Be not forever nurtured, but nurture.
And bring the children of your love
    through your motherhood
To the Mother Church.
And together, as mothers and mothered,
Giving and receiving, receiving and giving,
Each to oneself and others in their proper time,
You, your children and Mother Church will journey
    to the kingdom
Of Heaven, with mother, as mothers.

Topics for Personal Exploration
Alone or in Small Group-Sharing

Bringing the Mother with You
1. How did you react to the title of this book?
2. When have you felt most motherless?
3. When have you felt mothered by your own mother or other mother-figures in your life?
4. What are your present sources of nurturing?
5. What qualities do you take from your mother and what do you resist taking?
6. Write an unsent letter to your mother about the above. What might she reply?
7. Do you play a mothering role now? To whom?
8. How do you respond to the image of Mother Mary?
9. Trace the history of the growth and/or decrease of your personal devotion to Mary. What was the moment you felt closest to her? furthest from her?
10. In what ways does Mary seem to you an appropriate model for modern women? an inappropriate one?
11. Write all the songs or prayers to Mary you can recall or find. Note your feelings.

The Annunciation : Living with Surprise
1. List the joyful surprises in your life. Describe your favorite in detail.

2. List the painful surprises in your life.
3. How have these closed you up to surprise?
4. What do you fear most from the future?
5. How do you make room in the future for surprise?
6. How long does it take you to surrender to new things in your life?
7. Are there any new elements in the present you have not surrendered to?
8. How do you accept, understand, or fight the Church's stance about openness to accepting a pregnancy that comes as a surprise? Are you too afraid of losing control over your life to risk exploring the natural methods?

The Visitation : Giving and Seeking Support
1. Think of peak moments when you affirmed a friend or were yourself confirmed by one.
2. Describe the moment when you were in deepest need of affirmation from someone.
3. Who in your family is most confirming?
4. Are you free enough to tell your secrets to your friends?
5. "Sisterhood is powerful," the feminists remind us. In what ways is this illustrated by the Visitation?
6. In what ways are you driven to "accomplishment" at the expense of not being present to others?
7. What helps you share from the heart, rather than merely factually or intellectually?
8. Recall instances when a stranger confirmed you.
9. Write a confirming statement about each significant person in your life and share this with them when appropriate.

Nativity : Creating the New
1. Have you ever witnessed a childbirth? Describe your experience.
2. Write a re-creation of your own birth as you imagine it.
3. Describe your own childbirth(s) if you are a mother.
4. If you have never borne a child, describe your feelings about this fact. What have you "mothered or fathered forth?"

112

5. What is the most creative thing you've ever done?
6. List several creative projects you would like to be part of before you die. How do you deal with those who belittle your creativity as hobby?
7. Have you known anyone who lost a baby? How would you comfort such a woman? If you have ever lost a child, write this infant a letter.
8. Have you known anyone who shared with you that she had an abortion? Were you able to support her personhood and that of her lost baby? How do you see the Church trying to protect the personhood of both infant and mother in rejecting abortion?
9. Have you breast-fed your child? Describe your experience. If not, how do you respond to the image of a woman breast-feeding?

Presentation : Handing on the Tradition
1. What family rituals were part of your life as a child?
2. Which have you discarded and which have you carried on?
3. Which rituals have you started yourself?
4. Do you help arrange family celebrations or is it all left to you, or one other person?
5. Describe your most profound experiences of ritual, whether familial (a Thanksgiving dinner); or ecclesial: baptism, confirmation, penance, marriage, ordination, anointing, Eucharist.
6. Do you have personal rituals to enhance your sense of the sacred?
7. Simeon and Anna lived with great longing. List the longings you feel most intensely now — personal, familial, national, global. What is your central longing?

The Finding in the Temple : Losing and Keeping
1. Were you ever lost as a child? Recall the joy of seeing your parents.
2. Describe that moment or that period in your life when you felt most lost.

3. List the people whom you have lost from your life by death or time's decay. What was the gift each person gave you? Write a letter or a dialogue with the person whom you miss most. Keep writing and praying until you have a sense of this person's presence.
4. Jesus talked with the scholars. What dialogue do you keep with writers and teachers? What teacher did you have who was most helpful to you?
5. Is there any book that you were hardly able to put down? What part of your soul did it touch?
6. In your parental roles, describe the struggle with the process of letting your children go and receiving them back on a new level.
7. Do you like your work? Write a fantasy of exactly what Joseph would say to you were he teaching you about your work.
8. Do you have difficulty accepting petty daily tasks? Can you find splendor in the ordinary?

The Agony in the Garden : Crying Out
1. Recall the most agonizing moment of your life. Were you too stoical in confronting your agony?
2. Were you able to ask for help from others at that time? from God?
3. Have you ever been the one to comfort another in their agony?
4. Write a dialogue with Jesus about healing the memory of an agony where you were left alone.
5. What is the difficult cup of sorrow you are struggling to accept now?
6. When have you been angered by someone's telling you to obey God's will? Was their admonition helpful or not? Do you have difficulty obeying legitimate human authorities?
7. When have you ever experienced peace from praying, "Not my will, but thine be done?"

The Scourging : Enduring Violence
1. What is the greatest violence you have done toward anyone?

2. What is the greatest violence done to you?

3. Describe how you are violent toward yourself and others in your present circumstances.

4. Have you ever thought of God as being violent toward you? Describe your feelings about that.

5. In what ways do you need to become more violent about besieging the kingdom of God (i.e., "the kingdom of heaven suffers violence and the violent bear it away").

6. When do you think people should be passive? assertive? aggressive? Do you believe that assertiveness or aggressiveness can be combined with unconditional love?

The Crowning of Thorns : Accepting Humiliation

1. Recall those times in your life when you felt most humilated and mocked.

2. Describe any moments of reconciliation with people you thought had humiliated you.

3. List people who have humiliated you. Focus on one person whom you most need to forgive, describing the circumstances that surrounded his/her life at this time which help explain the action toward you. Write an imaginary letter to the person or dialogue with him/her until you have a sense of some resolution.

4. When has your agony led you to a resignation that refuses to hope?

5. What are some unloving aspects of your relationships with your intimates (spouse or friends) that you have refused to accept, or resigned yourself to in a way that precludes hope?

The Carrying of the Cross : Flowing with Pain

1. When has pain seemed unendurable to you?

2. Was there a Simeon to help you with this cross or a Veronica to wipe your face?

3. Are there those who have let you down whom you need to forgive? Describe the situation and write a dialogue with that person.

4. Do you find it hard to forgive yourself when you fall under your burdens?

5. Have you ever fled from ties that seemed too burdensome?
6. What do you use to tranquilize yourself from pain: drugs? alcohol? overwork? other?
7. List the sources you have which enable you to bear more than you think you can.

The Crucifixion : Relating to the End
1. Write a description of what you would like your dying to be like. Who would you like there? What would you like your last words to be?
2. If you have witnessed a death, describe this event and your feelings about it.
3. Have you ever been able to experience yourself as so united to God that you could relate to everyone, even "enemies," with His love?
4. Go through the last words of Jesus and make them your own by remembering the moments in which you have experienced similar realities. (For example, what would you will your friends in the way that Jesus gave Mary to John and John to Mary.)
5. Write a fantasy in which death comes to you as a mother calling you home. Tell her your fears; hear her answers.

The Resurrection : Touching Again
1. Make a list of beautiful things your hands have touched. Describe in detail your most profound experience of touching or being touched.
2. Have you ever been comforted by the touch of a stranger?
3. In your family were you free to touch? Are you inclined to snuggle close to others or keep a distance?
4. Recall peak experiences of being comforted by touching.
5. Do you fear that any physical contact can become sexually illicit?
6. Are you moving now towards greater or less touching?
7. The Church has always used touching in her rituals—anointing, blessing. What is your feeling about the kiss of peace? Touching strangers? Germs from the chalice?

116

8. What is your favorite scriptural account of Jesus touching someone?
9. Have you ever been "grabbed" instead of touched? You yourself grabbed, not touched? How do you elicit and guard tenderness in touching?
10. Make a list of "deaths" in your life—inner and outer events that brought mourning and loss. Then list what gift of resurrection came, if it did so.
11. What are the "old forms" in your relationships to family, work, and Church that you have difficulty letting go of. Dialogue with Jesus about this.

The Ascension : Coming Home
1. When have you pursued emotional or spiritual thrills in the fear that God's eternal promises will be false? What was the result?
2. Recall those moments when you wished that you could just enjoy this life without having to seek the eternal dimension. What changed this wish?
3. Do you see your own body as beautiful? That of the opposite sex?
4. List some important body memories from childhood, adolescence, and adulthood. Then write a letter to your body describing how you feel about being with it for all eternity. Do you feel it is worthy of eternity?
5. List the moment in your life when you have experienced "glory."
6. Write a fantasy about whom you would like to meet in heaven.
7. List ten main periods in your life. Then try to label whether they were a period of earth, air, fire, or water. What sort of period are you in now?

The Descent of the Holy Spirit : Loving Unconditionally
1. Recall rooms where you have locked yourself away in fear.
2. What rooms within you now need unlocking, warming, loosening by the Spirit?

3. Have you ever experienced being loved unconditionally by anyone? Describe this person who so love(s)d you.
4. List the reasons you won't love yourself unconditionally. Write a dialogue with the Holy Spirit about this list.
5. When have you been conscious of receiving a gift of the Holy Spirit? When of rejecting it?
6. Recall when you have experienced the Church as a homeland of hearts.
7. Do you see yourself as a comforter or a crusader in the Church?
8. Do you think of those who choose differently from you in this regard as threats or comrades?

The Assumption : Bringing Mother Home

1. Why do you think the Church's tradition has placed such emphasis on the *bodily* aspects of the mysteries of the Assumption, Resurrection, Ascension?
2. What are your feelings about the new emphasis on body consciousness? Describe someone you know (of) who focuses on this issue. Do you think concentration on physical development is partly a compensation for loss of faith in eternal fulfillment?
3. Describe someone you know who has little consciousness of his/her body.
4. The psychiatrist C.W. Jung said that the most momentous event of the twentieth century was the declaration of the doctrine of Mary's Assumption in 1950 because it meant that a new understanding of the importance of the feminine principle was dawning for modern man. Do you agree or disagree? What signs of this new consciousness do you see? Would you like to see?
5. The radical feminists insist, "my body belongs to me." The Christian feminist counters, "my body belongs to God and me." Write a letter to a radical feminist explaining the latter quotation.
6. On what occasions in your life have you had to let go of a childish desire to be without stain of sin? Write a prayer to Our

Lady turning over a list of all the things you try to be perfect about. In what way can one strive to grow in goodness without becoming obsessed with guilty self-hatred?

The Crowning of Mary Queen of Heaven :
Hope Brought Full Circle
1. Select one of the titles of Our Lady and reflect on its meaning for you. Which of your needs does it speak to?
2. Make a list of homecomings in your life. Describe in detail the most moving.
3. Recall some time when you had some honor, admiration, or love publicly extended to you. Did you find it hard or easy to accept?
4. Recall when you had a party or ceremony honoring someone. How did they receive this attention? Did you have difficulty letting them take center stage?
5. Write a fantasy describing what you would do if you were queen — how would you dress, walk, speak.
6. Read the Magnificat, which Mary sang at the Visitation; write the song Mary would sing as queen about her journey, her homecoming, her joy.
7. Can you believe in fullness for you? for the cosmos? What are your images of eternity?

How to Meditate on the Mysteries of the Rosary

THE MYSTERIES

(Meditate on each of these themes for a decade of the Rosary.)

Joyful (Monday, Thursday,
   Sundays of Advent-through Epiphany)
Annunciation
Visitation
Nativity
Presentation
Finding in the Temple
Sorrowful (Tuesday, Friday,
   Sundays of Lent)
The Garden
Scourging
Crowning with Thorns
Carrying the Cross
Crucifixion
Glorious (Wednesday, Saturday,
   Sundays after Easter)
Resurrection
Ascension
Descent of the Holy Spirit
Assumption
Crowning of Mary Queen of Heaven

Creed (prayed while viewing the crucifix)
I believe in God, the Father Almighty, Creator of Heaven and earth; and in Jesus Christ, His only Son, our Lord; Who was conceived by the Holy Ghost, born of the Virgin Mary, suffered under Pontius Pilate, was crucified, died, and was buried. He descended into hell; The third day He rose again from the dead; He ascended

into heaven; and sitteth on the right hand of God, the Father Almighty; from hence He shall come to judge the quick and the dead. I believe in the Holy Ghost, the holy Catholic Church, the Communion of Saints, the Forgiveness of sins, the Resurrection of the body, and the life everlasting. Amen.

The Our Father (prayed on the larger beads) Our Father, who art in heaven, hallowed be Thy Name; Thy kingdom come; Thy will be done on earth as it is in heaven. Give us this day our daily bread; and forgive us our trespasses as we forgive those who trespass against us; and lead us not into temptation, but deliver us from evil. Amen.

The Hail Mary (prayed on small beads) Hail Mary, full of grace! The Lord is with you; blessed are you among women, and blessed is the fruit of your womb, Jesus. Holy Mary, mother of God, pray for us sinners, now and at the hour of our death. Amen.